CW00640894

RECIPES
FOR YOUNG
VEGETARIANS

RECIPES FOR YOUNG VEGETARIANS

SAMMY GREEN

foulsham

LONDON • NEW YORK • TORONTO • SYDNEY

foulsham

The Publishing House

Bennetts Close, Cippenham, Berkshire SL1 5AP

ISBN 0-572-02113-5

Copyright © 1995 Sammy Green

All rights reserved

The Copyright Act (1956) prohibits (subject to certain
very limited exceptions) the making of copies of
any copyright work or of a substantial part of such
a work, including the making of copies by
photocopying or similar process. Written
permission to make a copy or copies must
therefore normally be obtained from the publisher
in advance. It is advisable also to consult the
publisher if in any doubt as to the legality of any
copying which is to be undertaken.

Phototypeset in Great Britain by Typesetting Solutions, Slough, Berks.
Printed in Great Britain by
Cox & Wyman Ltd, Reading, Berkshire

contents

Why Wholefoods? Why Vegetarian?   7

Is a Vegetarian Diet Healthy for the Young?   11

The Vegetarian Kitchen   15

The Ingredients   17

Finger on the Pulse   19

Brighter Breakfasts   21

Filling Feasts   37

Sweet Surprises   83

The Cookie Jar   107

Cook Your Own   119

Friends to Tea   137

Drinks   149

Index   157

why wholefoods?
WHY VEGETARIAN?

w holefoods are quite simply foods with nothing added and nothing taken away. Cooking the whole-food way means no more refined ingredients and no more chemicals. Refined foods have developed over the years because people demanded finer textures and clean white colours. As a result of this we became accustomed to eating only white rice, white flour, white sugar and white bread. What people did not realise was that to obtain these products they had to throw away all the goodness contained in the food in its natural state.

As well as refining foods, we have developed methods of preserving and altering their taste using chemical additives. These chemicals also take the form of fertilizers and sprays used on crops, and hormones and antibiotics injected into livestock. By eating these products we are eating chemicals which our bodies not only to not require but may even find harmful.

We know for sure that the use of these foods causes problems from the health point of view, which is why modern governments are encouraging us to review our eating habits. A good percentage of hospital beds would be lying empty, and the money saved could be spent elsewhere, if we all paid heed to the latest medical findings in relation to the food we eat.

It is for these reasons, as well as for the obvious humane aspect of vegetarianism, that a lot of young people are rejecting meat. Parents should admire their decision and learn from their wisdom. Committed vegetarian families will, I hope, find the recipes in this book exciting, and for those setting out on this new path, I hope they will help us to make the transition easier.

Why No Salt?

Salt serves no useful purpose other than flavouring food. All the salt our bodies need can be obtained from eating natural foods. Doctors believe that too much salt can cause the body to retain more water, putting extra strain on the heart and kidneys. This does not mean that a wholefood diet is bland and tasteless; it is just the opposite. Nature herself has provided us with hundreds of herbs and spices, many of which have been neglected due to our obsession with the salt cellar.

Why No Sugar?

Sugar not only helps to rot your teeth and make you fat, but it is also responsible for a number of diseases in our society. Sugar is a form of drug – the more you have, the more you want. How many of us never eat sweets but, given one chocolate, we feel the urge to devour the whole box? Giving up sugar does not mean giving up sweet foods or running short on energy, despite the claims of some chocolate manufacturers. Fresh and dried fruits will provide the sweetness, and bread, potatoes and cereals the energy.

Why Less Fat?

Fats are associated with many diseases today. Too much fat can quite simply cloud the blood and block up the arteries. Our bodies require a certain amount of fats but these need not be the harmful hard animal fats.

Why More Fibre?

The importance of fibre has only been realized in recent years because of the huge increase in consumption of 'fast' processed, convenience foods. At the same time, doctors have recorded large increases in the numbers of people suffering from constipation and related diseases. When sufferers changed their eating habits to include more natural foods the symptoms disappeared.

Fibre is the bulky part of the food which we have become used to discarding. Extra fibre means that waste products can be carried through our bodies much more quickly. Studies have shown that the average Western body can take up to 100 hours to move waste through it, compared with 35 hours in African tribesmen living off fibre-rich grains and pulses. The African tribesmen are also free of all diseases related to a low-fibre diet.

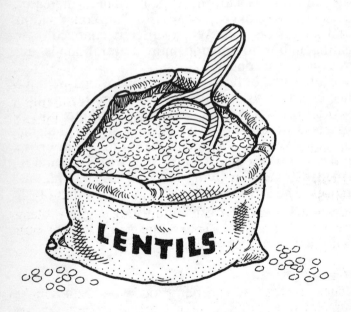

C H A P T E R 2

is a vegetarian diet healthy for THE YOUNG?

|t| he simple answer to this question is an unequivocal 'yes'. As long as the diet is varied and wholesome there is no cause for concern.

For healthy growth we all require carbohydrates, proteins, fats, vitamins and minerals. Problems only arise when a proper balance of all these is not maintained. The latest recommendations are that a balanced diet should be 15% protein, 30-35% fat and 40-50% carbohydrate. All these components are to be found in a vegetarian diet.

Proteins
These are essential for growth and repair, and growing youngsters require more than adults. Protein-rich foods are pulses (beans, peas and lentils), nuts and dairy produce (including eggs).

Carbohydrates
These are long-acting energy foods and should make up 50% of our daily intake. Carbohydrate foods are

wholewheat bread, cereals, grains, brown pasta and potatoes. Collectively, these are the 'complex' carbohydrates. There is a second group of carbohydrates known as 'simple' carbohydrates and these are the refined sugar products. They supply instant energy but no nutrients and leave you feeling tired. They should therefore be shunned. A body which has sufficient stores of complex carbohydrates has all the energy it needs.

Fats

Fats are the most concentrated form of energy and are essential for the absorption of vitamins and minerals. They also help to regulate body temperature and protect vital organs. The fats which we should avoid are the 'saturated' fats because they contain cholesterol which is thought to be a major contributory factor of heart disease. Heart disease may not concern you now, but cholesterol takes years to build up in the arteries, so we must encourage good habits in our children as early as possible. Saturated fat is found in all animal fats, egg yolks and hard cheeses.

The fats we should be using are the 'polyunsaturated' vegetable oil variety, such as soya, safflower, sesame (benne), sunflower and corn oils.

Vitamins

There are two types of vitamins – water soluble and fat soluble. The fat soluble vitamins can be stored in the body and include:

Vitamin A found in milk, cheese, margarine, eggs, dark leafy vegetables, carrots and tomatoes. It is essential for sight and protein metabolism.

Vitamin D found in milk, butter, eggs, cheese and yoghurt. It is essential for healthy bones and teeth.

Vitamin E found in margarine, wholewheat bread, cereals, wheatgerm and eggs. It helps in metabolism.

Vitamin K found in green leafy vegetables. It is required for healthy blood clotting.

Water soluble vitamins cannot be stored in the body and are often lost in the cooking water. They are:

Vitamin C is found in citrus fruits, tomatoes, green leafy vegetables and potatoes. It helps in the fight against infection and in the absorption of iron.

Vitamin B is found in yeast, pulses, whole grains, rice, milk, eggs, green vegetables, wheatgerm and peanuts. It is responsible for a healthy nervous system.

Minerals

Iron is important for the production of healthy blood. It is usually kept in high supply if a varied diet is eaten, but young girls should ensure they eat plenty of iron-rich foods because they lose iron when menstruating. Iron is found in eggs, flour, bread, black treacle, beans, peas, spinach and dried fruits.

Calcium is needed for strong bones and is present in milk, cheese, eggs, bread, flour, yoghurt and green vegetables.

CHAPTER 3

the vegetarian KITCHEN

W hen cooking the vegetarian way you will use ingredients which may require a little extra preparation. Most kitchens will already be equipped with graters and sharp knives. There are, however, a number of useful gadgets which will help you to cut down on the time spent in preparation and cooking.

A food processor is a great asset for all those salads and vegetables, enabling you to produce almost instant raw vegetable dishes.

A blender will turn leftovers into nutritious soups and sauces. Ground nuts and puréed beans will be no problem.

A wok is a must for all those stir-fry vegetarian meals. It is a marvellous method of cooking, producing crisp vegetables with the minimum of fat and fuss.

A pressure cooker will cut the cooking time for all those beans. I have only recently acquired mine and wonder how I managed without it.

A large slotted spoon will come in useful for skimming off the froth which forms when boiling beans.

A large sieve (strainer) will also come in handy when sorting through grains and beans.

the INGREDIENTS

h ere are some useful tips on the various ingredients which are used in vegetarian cooking.

Grains
Always use whole grains and cook them until just tender. Ring the changes, using wheat, barley or buckwheat grains instead of the usual rice. Experiment with millet, bulgar or couscous, adding them to casseroles and soups.

Flour
If you are introducing wholewheat flour to your family, start slowly, mixing white with brown to begin with. The ultimate aim is 100% wholewheat but it may take time. Stoneground flour is the traditional method of grinding the grain between two stones. The resulting flour tastes much more wholesome.

Nuts and Seeds
Years ago people used to laugh at the 'nut cutlet', but not any more. Nuts can be eaten on their own or used

to produce roasts, stews, salads, etc. Use seeds to enrich your baking or for crunchy savoury toppings. Both also make ideal snack foods, although whole nuts are not suitable for children under five as they could choke.

Oils
Avoid oils from animal sources. The best oils are those which are cold-pressed because they retain the vitamins lost through heat during the manufacture of ordinary oils. They are slightly more expensive but rather nice to keep for salads.

Pulses
Do experiment with the full range and, if the family is reluctant, try grinding the beans first to add as a powder to dishes. That way they won't even notice they are eating beans.

Fruits and Vegetables
Always buy these as fresh as possible because they lose nutrients very rapidly once picked. When cooking, use the minimum of water and cook until just tender. Do not add soda or salt to the cooking water. Always use the cooking water to make soups, sauces and gravies, because that is where many of the vitamins are after cooking.

Nowadays, the majority of fruit and vegetables are sprayed with chemicals. Those that are not are labelled 'organic' and are just beginning to appear in many of the more enlightened supermarkets. They may cost slightly more, but is there a price on good health?

Don't always feel you must serve vegetables cooked. A raw meal a day is much more nutritious than crisps and sweets.

finger on **THE PULSE**

p ulses are the seeds of legumes, and include beans, peas and lentils. Our older relatives regard them as second class proteins but we now know that they provide use with just as much protein as meat. Consequently, they've been promoted to the rather grand title of 'first class'. They are first class too in the variety of dishes you can prepare with them, and in the low cost of buying them.

One small nutritional point to remember is that a meal of pulses on their own is incomplete as it does not contain the full range of amino acids. However, it is a simple matter to correct this. To form complete protein all you have to do is ensure that you serve pulses with grains, dairy produce, wholewheat flour, nuts or seeds. You will probably find that this happens quite naturally, beans on toast being a classic example.

Cooking Pulses

All pulses, except peas and lentils, require overnight soaking. To cut time, place the beans in boiling water and leave for an hour. Drain and replace the water. Boil until tender according to the chart below.

Freezing
Beans freeze well. Cook large quantities, package in 450 g/1 lb bags and freeze, ready for instant bean dishes.

Guide to Cooking Pulses
The chart shows approximate boiling times for 225 g/8 oz/½ lb beans after soaking. The exact cooking time depends on the freshness of the beans.

First, wash the beans thoroughly and soak overnight. Drain and cover with fresh cold water to cook.

	Boiling Time	*Pressure Cooker*
Adzuki	1-1½ hours	20 minutes
Black-eyed	1 hour	10 minutes
Butter (cannellini)	1½ hours	20 minutes
Haricot (navy)	1-1½ hours	15 minutes
Pinto	1½ hours	20 minutes
Soya	2-3 hours	30 minutes
Red kidney	1-1½ hours	20 minutes
Mung	45 minutes	8 minutes
Chick-peas	1½ hours	20 minutes
Flagolet	1½ hours	20 minutes

The following do not require soaking:

Red lentils	30 minutes	
Green and brown lentils	1 hour	
Split peas	1 hour	

brighter BREAKFASTS

t he first meal of the day is also the most important. It is the meal which tops up the energy supply to carry a young person through the morning.

From my years in teaching, I remember being able to spot the youngsters who had not found time to eat a breakfast. They were the ones who lolled over their desks, yawned through lessons and appeared generally lethargic and tired. Admittedly late nights were a contributory factor but so too were missed breakfasts.

There is no need to go to elaborate lengths to provide cooked food, nor to worry too much about protein at this meal. The important thing is to provide carbohydrate for energy. Offer youngsters a choice of bread, cereals and yoghurt and keep the fruit bowl topped up with really fresh fruit.

Adolescents are a particularly difficult group and many parents fight losing battles with slimming daughters and uncooperative sons. For those youngsters, keep a supply of healthy snacks, such as peanuts or dried fruits, which they may eat on the way out of the door!

sultana porridge

Serves 4

Ingredients	Metric	Imperial	American
Skimmed milk or soya milk	*600 ml*	*1 pint*	*2½ cups*
Vanilla essence	*½ tps*	*½ tsp*	*½ tsp*
Sultanas (golden raisins)	*100 g*	*4 oz*	*⅔ cup*
Rolled oats	*50 g*	*2 oz*	*½ cup*

1.   Pour the milk into a saucepan and stir in the vanilla essence and sultanas. Heat gently and, when it begins to boil, stir in the oats.

2.   Simmer the porridge gently for 4–5 minutes, stirring continuously, until thick.

3.   Serve hot with a little maple syrup or honey.

Did you know?
The original Scots porridge was made with oatmeal and water and eaten with salt!

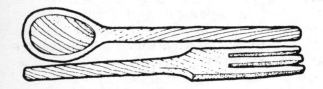

semolina smoothie

Serves 4

Ingredients	Metric	Imperial	American
Skimmed milk or soya milk	600 ml	1 pint	2½ cups
Wholewheat semolina	50 g	2 oz	⅓ cup
Free-range egg, beaten	1	1	1
Clear honey	2 tbsp	2 tbsp	2 tbsp
Apricot purée	300 ml	½ pint	1¼ cups
Toasted flaked (slivered) almonds	25 g	1 oz	¼ cup

1.   Heat the milk into a saucepan and sprinkle on the semolina. Bring to the boil, then reduce the heat and simmer gently for 3–4 minutes, stirring occasionally to prevent sticking.
2.   Remove from the heat and stir in the egg and honey. Mix well, then leave to cool covered with a damp cloth to prevent a skin forming.
3.   When cool, divide half the semolina between four tall glasses. Cover with a layer of apricot purée, then top with the remaining semolina. Sprinkle on the toasted almonds and serve chilled.

Did you know?
Semolina is the starch from wheat and therefore a valuable energy source.

yummie yoghurts

Serves 4

Ingredients	Metric	Imperial	American
Skimmed milk	*600 ml*	*1 pint*	*2½ cups*
Live plain yoghurt	*1 tbsp*	*1 tbsp*	*1 tbsp*
Chopped fresh fruit			
of your choice	*100 g*	*4 oz*	*1 cup*
Honey	*1 tbsp*	*1 tbsp*	*1 tbsp*
Wheatgerm	*1 tsp*	*1 tsp*	*1 tsp*

1. Fill a wide-necked thermos flask with boiling water and leave to warm.
2. Meanwhile, bring the milk to boiling point in a saucepan, then leave to cool, stirring occasionally to prevent a skin forming.
3. When the milk is hand-hot add the yoghurt and stir well. Pour the water out of the flask and fill with the yoghurt and milk mixture. Cover and leave to stand for 6–12 hours in a warm place (the airing cupboard is ideal).
4. Stir in the chosen fruit, honey and wheatgerm. Chill in the refrigerator before serving.

Did you know?
Commercial fruit yoghurts can be almost 18% refined sugar. Yummie Yoghurts may also be made in an electric yoghurt-making machine.

granola

Children love the crunchy texture of this breakfast dish.

Serves 4-5

Ingredients	Metric	Imperial	American
Sunflower oil	*120 ml*	*4 fl oz*	*½ cup*
Honey	*75 g*	*3 oz*	*¼ cup*
Vanilla essence	*2 tsp*	*2 tsp*	*2 tsp*
Rolled oats	*450 g*	*1 lb*	*4¾ cups*
Sunflower seeds	*50 g*	*2 oz*	*½ cup*
Sesame (benne) seeds	*25 g*	*1 oz*	*¼ cup*
Desiccated (shredded) coconut	*50 g*	*2 oz*	*⅔ cup*
Unsalted peanuts	*50 g*	*2 oz*	*¼ cup*
Wholewheat flour	*75 g*	*3 oz*	*¾ cup*

1.   Mix together the oil, honey and vanilla in a saucepan and heat gently until the honey has dissolved. Stir in the remaining ingredients.

2.   Spread the mixture evenly in greased baking trays and bake in a preheated oven at 170°C/325°F/Gas Mark 3 for about 15 minutes, or until golden brown. Stir occasionally to ensure even colouring. Leave to cool.

3.   When cold, store the Granola in an airtight container. Serve with favourite dried fruits.

Did you know?
Cereals are a major source of fibre. A high-fibre diet will protect against many of our western diseases.

spiced grapefruit

Serves 2

Ingredients	Metric	Imperial	American
Large, juicy grapefruit	*1*	*1*	*1*
Apple juice concentrate	*2 tbsp*	*2 tbsp*	*2 tbsp*
Grated rind of 1 small			
lemon			
Mixed spice	*½ tsp*	*½ tsp*	*½ tsp*
Wholewheat breadcrumbs	*1 tbsp*	*1 tbsp*	*1 tbsp*

1.   Cut the grapefruit in half. Using a very sharp knife, cut between the membranes to loosen the fruit segments.

2.   Mix together the apple juice, lemon rind and mixed spice. Pour over each grapefruit and sprinkle with breadcrumbs.

3.   Place the grapefruit halves under a hot grill (broiler) for 10 minutes until browned and bubbling. Serve immediately.

Did you know?
There are at least 30 varieties of grapefruit and its high vitamin C content is rivalled only by the orange.

Apple juice concentrate makes a good natural substitute for sugar. It is available from health-food shops and some supermarkets.

orange oatcakes

Makes 15

Ingredients	Metric	Imperial	American
Oatmeal	225 g	8 oz	1⅓ cups
Plain (all-purpose) wholewheat flour	100 g	4 oz	1 cup
Baking powder	1 tsp	1 tsp	1 tsp
Grated rind and juice of 1 small orange			
Vegetable margarine	50 g	2 oz	¼ cup
Skimmed milk or soya milk			

1.   Mix the oatmeal, flour, baking powder and orange rind together in a bowl. Add the margarine and rub (cut) in.

2.   Place the orange juice in a measuring jug and make up to 150 ml/¼ pint/⅔ cup with milk. Pour into the oat mixture, mix to a firm dough and knead lightly.

3.   Place the dough on a floured board and roll out to 5 mm/¼ inch thick. Using a 5 cm/21 inch pastry cutter cut out 15 oatcakes.

4.   Place the oatcakes on greased baking sheets and bake in a preheated oven at 200°C/400°F/ Gas Mark 6 for 20 minutes.

5.   Cool on a wire rack and serve with orange marmalade.

Did you know?
Oats are 13% protein.

muesli munch

Serves 4-5

Ingredients	Metric	Imperial	American
Rolled oats	100 g	4 oz	1 cup
Barley flakes	50 g	2 oz	½ cup
Wheat flakes	50 g	2 oz	½ cup
Raisins	25 g	1 oz	3 tbsp
Sultanas (golden raisins)	25 g	1 oz	3 tbsp
Currants	25 g	1 oz	3 tbsp
Eating apple, cored and grated	1	1	1
Banana, sliced	1	1	1
Unsalted peanuts	50 g	2 oz	¼ cup

1. Mix all the dry ingredients together in a large bowl.
2. Add all the fruit and nuts and serve with either skimmed milk, plain yoghurt or orange juice.

Note
Larger quantities of the basic dried mix, without the fresh fruit, can be made and stored in an airtight container. Try varying the fresh fruits added, according to the season. For a softer consistency, soak overnight before serving.

Did you know?
The original Muesli consisted only of oats and grated apple and was invented by a Swiss – Dr Bircher Benner.

hot banana fingers

Serves 5

Ingredients	Metric	Imperial	American
Skimmed milk or soya milk	120 ml	4 fl oz	½ cup
Honey	1 tsp	1 tsp	1 tsp
Free-range eggs	2	2	2
Banana, sliced	1	1	1
Thick slices wholewheat bread	5	5	5
Sunflower oil	1 tbsp	1 tbsp	1 tbsp

1.   Blend together the milk, honey, eggs and banana in a blender or food processor. Pour into a shallow dish.
2.   Cut the bread into finger-sized pieces and dip each one into the batter, making sure that all sides are well coated.
3.   Heat the oil in a frying pan (skillet) and fry the banana fingers quickly until crisp and golden.

Did you know?
We should try to restrict out total egg consumption to three per week, so do not allow a greedy youngster to gobble up all these Banana fingers in one go!

morning muffins

These delicious muffins, served warm with apple spread, will guarantee the children don't run short of energy mid-morning.

Serves 4

Ingredients	Metric	Imperial	American
Cornmeal	*225 g*	*8 oz*	*1½ cups*
Wholewheat flour	*50 g*	*2 oz*	*½ cup*
Baking powder	*1½ tsp*	*1½ tsp*	*1½ tsp*
Skimmed milk or			
soya milk	*300 ml*	*½ pint*	*1¼ cups*
Apple juice concentrate	*1½ tbsp*	*1½ tbsp*	*1½ tbsp*
Vanilla extract	*½ tsp*	*½ tsp*	*½ tsp*
Free-range egg whites	*2*	*2*	*2*

1. Mix all the dry ingredients together in a large bowl. Stir in the milk, apple juice and vanilla and beat thoroughly.
2. Whisk the egg whites until stiff and gently fold into the mixture.
3. Spoon into a greased bun tray (muffin pan) and bake in a preheated oven at 200°C/400°F/Gas Mark 6 for 20 minutes.

Did you know?
Skimmed milk contains as much calcium as full milk.

tangerine and rice breakfast

This sustaining breakfast is best made with soya milk because the result is creamier than with cows' milk. Make the rice the night beforee and reheat the next morning.

Serves 4

Ingredients	Metric	Imperial	American
Soya milk	600 ml	1 pint	2½ cups
Water	150 ml	¼ pint	⅔ cup
Honey	1 tbsp	1 tbsp	1 tbsp
Grated orange rind	2 tsp	2 tsp	2 tsp
Grated nutmeg	1 tsp	1 tsp	1 tsp
Short-grain brown rice	225 g	8 oz	½ lb
Tangerines, peeled	4	4	4
Sesame (benne) seeds	1 tbsp	1 tbsp	1 tbsp

1.   Mix together the milk, water, honey, orange rind and nutmeg in a large saucepan and stir in the rice. Bring to the boil, then lower the heat and simmer for 45 minutes, stirring occasionally, until the liquid is absorbed and the rice is tender. Remove from the heat.

2.   Divide each tangerine into segments and place in the bottom of four individual dishes. Pour a portion of rice over each, sprinkle with the sesame seeds and serve hot.

Did you know?
Brown rice is a rich source of B vitamins, especially B_1, as well as vitamin E, phosphorus, calcium and iron. White rice contains none of these.

egg and pea scramble

A much more exciting version of plain
scrambled eggs.

Serves 2

Ingredients	Metric	Imperial	American
Free-range eggs	*3*	*3*	*3*
Skimmed milk or soya milk	*2 tbsp*	*2 tbsp*	*2 tbsp*
Chopped fresh mint or chives	*2 tsp*	*2 tsp*	*2 tsp*
Cooked green peas	*50 g*	*2 oz*	*⅓ cup*
Vegetable margarine for cooking			

1.   In a small bowl, whisk together the eggs, milk
and mint or chives. Add the peas and whisk
again.

2.   Melt a little margarine in a small saucepan
and pour in the egg mixture. Cook gently until set,
stirring occasionally to prevent sticking.

3.   Served piled on thick slices of wholewheat
bread or toast.

Did you know?
Eggs from battery hens have been found to be low
in vitamin B_{12} and essential fatty acids.

sunday brunch

Serves 4-5

Ingredients	Metric	Imperial	American
Wholewheat bread	*225 g*	*8 oz*	*½ lb*
Free-range eggs	*2*	*2*	*2*
Cheddar cheese, grated	*175 g*	*6 oz*	*1½ cups*
Skimmed milk or			
soya milk	*600 ml*	*1 pint*	*2½ cups*
Plain yoghurt	*1 tbsp*	*1 tbsp*	*1 tbsp*
Chopped fresh parsley	*1 tbsp*	*1 tbsp*	*1 tbsp*
Tomatoes, sliced	*3*	*3*	*3*

1. Cut the bread into 1.5 cm/½ inch cubes and place in a bowl.
2. Whisk the eggs and pour over the bread. Stir in the cheese and place in the bottom of a 1.1 litre/2 pint ovenproof dish.
3. Heat the milk and yoghurt together until just warmed. Add the parsley and pour onto the bread mixture.
4. Arrange the tomato slices on top and bake in a preheated oven at 190°C/375°F/Gas Mark 5 for 45 minutes.
5. Serve with wholewheat toast.

Did you know?
Cheese is an excellent source of calcium, and there's more calcium in the body than any other mineral.

saturday savoury pancakes

Makes 4

Ingredients	Metric	Imperial	American
Plain (all-purpose) wholewheat flour	100 g	4 oz	1 cup
Free-range egg	1	1	1
Skimmed milk or soya milk	300 ml	½ pint	1¼ cups
Vegetable oil for frying			
Large onion, chopped	1	1	1
Large cooked potato, diced	1	1	1
Tomatoes, peeled and chopped	2	2	2
Soya sauce or tamari (see below)	1 tsp	1 tsp	1 tsp

1.   Place the flour in a large bowl and make a well in the centre. Break in the egg and gradually beat it into the flour.

2.   Gradually beat in the milk until a smooth batter forms. Leave to stand in a cool place for 30 minutes.

3.   Meanwhile, heat a little oil in a frying pan (skillet) and sauté the onion until transparent. Add the potato, tomatoes and soya sauce or tamari and heat through. Keep warm.

4.   Heat a little oil in a small frying pan (skillet) over a high heat. Add about 3 tbsp batter, turning the pan to coat the surface completely. Cook until the batter bubbles, then flip the pancake over.

Spread a quarter of the filling onto the pancake and fold over. Repeat to make another three pancakes. Serve hot.

Did you know?
Tamari or shoyu are made from soya beans but are superior to soya sauces which usually contain added sugar.

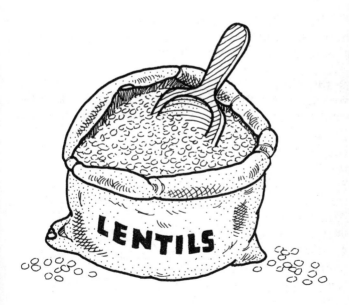

blender breakfast

This nourishing drink makes a high-energy start to the day for the young person who just cannot face eating breakfast.

Serves 1

Ingredients	Metric	Imperial	American
Skimmed milk or			
soya milk	*300 ml*	*½ pint*	*1¼ cups*
Banana, sliced	*1*	*1*	*1*
Wheatgerm	*1 tsp*	*1 tsp*	*1 tsp*
Clear honey	*1 tsp*	*1 tsp*	*1 tsp*

1. Place all the ingredients in a blender or food processor and blend until smooth. Pour into a tall glass and chill before serving.

Did you know?
Wheatgerm is the heart of the wheat grain and the most nutritious part. It is our richest source of vitamin E as well as B vitamins and phosphorus.

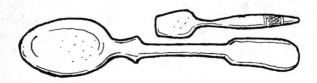

filling FEASTS

e veryone looks forward to the main meal of the day, whether it be at midday or in the evening. The vegetarian meal, because of its diversity of ingredients, should be just as tempting and appetizing as any other.

It is not only the adult gourmet who appreciates a well cooked and presented meal. I recall my young son watching me prepare a dinner party dish and asking, "Why don't you garnish *my* food?" From then on I remembered to add a twist of peel, a slice of lemon or a herb garnish to his plate.

To ring the changes, young people often enjoy meals served in bowls instead of on the usual plate, and a meal can be turned into something extra special just be serving a salad as an extra course instead of cooked vegetables. If you stay flexible and don't get too upset if your youngsters suddenly take a dislike to certain vegetables, you should be able to find a happy alternative. The main thing is to provide plenty of variety and you should not go too far wrong.

red lentil and apple knobs

Makes 8 small or 4 large

Ingredients	Metric	Imperial	American
Red lentils	225 g	8 oz	1 cup
Water	1.1 litres	2 pints	5 cups
Sunflower oil	2 tbsp	2 tbsp	2 tbsp
Finely chopped onion	1	1	1
Finely chopped apple	1	1	1
Cumin seeds	1 tsp	1 tsp	1 tsp
Wholewheat breadcrumbs	50 g	2 oz	1 cup
Grated carrot	1	1	1
Soya flour	25 g	1 oz	¼ cup
Vegetable extract	1 tsp	1 tsp	1 tsp
Cheddar cheese, grated	50 g	2 oz	½ cup

1. Wash the lentils and pick them over, discarding any stones or grit. Place in a large saucepan, cover with water and bring to the boil. Reduce the heat and simmer for about 30 minutes, or until the lentils are soft. Drain off any excess water.

2. Heat the oil in a frying pan (skillet) and sauté the onion until transparent. Add the apple and continue cooking for 3–4 minutes, or until just beginning to soften. Stir in the cumin seeds and cook for a further 2 minutes. Remove from the heat.

3. In a bowl, combine the breadcrumbs, lentils, grated carrot, soya flour and vegetable extract. Stir in the onion and apple and mix well.

4.   Spoon the mixture into eight greased bun tins (muffin pans) or four greased Yorkshire pudding tins (pans). Sprinkle on the cheese and bake in a preheated oven at 200°C/400°F/Gas Mark 6 for 30 minutes, or until golden brown.

Did you know?
The red lentil cooks quicker than other lentils because it has been split. Brown and green lentils are whole and therefore retain their shape.

Vegetable extract has a similar flavour to yeast extract and is used to flavour all kinds of savoury dishes.

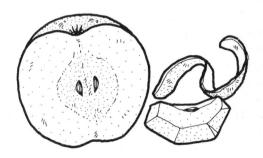

spaghetti bolognese

Serves 3-4

Ingredients	Metric	Imperial	American
Sunflower oil	*2 tbsp*	*2 tbsp*	*2 tbsp*
Onion, chopped	*1*	*1*	*1*
Carrot, diced	*1*	*1*	*1*
Celery stalk, diced	*1*	*1*	*1*
Small green (bell) pepper, seeded and diced	*½*	*½*	*½*
Mushrooms, sliced	*100 g*	*4 oz*	*1 cup*
Dried basil	*1 tsp*	*1 tsp*	*1 tsp*
Dried oregano	*1 tsp*	*1 tsp*	*1 tsp*
Tomato purée (paste)	*100 g*	*4 oz*	*½ cup*
Yeast extract	*1 tsp*	*1 tsp*	*1 tsp*
Canned tomatoes	*300 g*	*10 oz*	*2½ cups*
Cooked green or brown lentils (see page 20)	*100 g*	*4 oz*	*½ cup*
Wholewheat spaghetti	*225 g*	*8 oz*	*½ lb*
Grated Parmesan cheese, to taste			

1.   Heat the oil in a pan and sauté the onion until transparent. Add the carrot, celery and green pepper and cook over medium heat for 5 minutes, stirring continuously.

2.   Add the mushrooms and herbs and cook for a further 2 minutes.

3.   Mix the tomato purée, yeast extract and tomatoes together and add to the vegetables with the cooked lentils. (If the sauce is too thick, add a little hot vegetable stock or water.) Simmer gently for 15-20 minutes.

4.   Bring a large saucepan of water, with 1 tsp
sunflower oil added, to the boil and add the
spaghetti. Stir once, then boil for 15 minutes, or
until just soft. The easiest method of testing
spaghetti is to remove a strand and bite it.

5.   Drain well and pile onto warmed individual
plates. Top with a generous helping of the sauce.
Sprinkle on the Parmesan, if liked, and serve with a
large mixed salad.

Did you know?
One of Marco Polo's men, called Spaghetti, is
supposed to have pinched the recipe for pasta from
the Chinese.

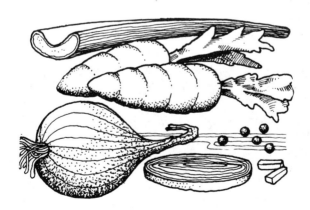

cauliflower crunch

Serves 4

Ingredients	Metric	Imperial	American
Large cauliflower,			
broken into florets	*1*	*1*	*1*
Vegetable margarine	*25 g*	*1 oz*	*2 tbsp*
Chopped onion	*1*	*1*	*1*
Wholewheat breadcrumbs	*175 g*	*6 oz*	*3 cups*
Rolled oats	*50 g*	*2 oz*	*½ cup*
Walnuts, chopped	*100 g*	*4 oz*	*1 cup*
Cheddar cheese, grated	*150 g*	*5 oz*	*1¼ cups*
Dried mixed herbs	*1 tsp*	*1 tsp*	*1 tsp*
Tomato purée (paste)	*1 tbsp*	*1 tbsp*	*1 tbsp*
Sauce			
Vegetable margarine	*100 g*	*4 oz*	*½ cup*
Wholewheat flour	*50 g*	*2 oz*	*½ cup*
Skimmed milk or			
soya milk	*600 ml*	*1 pint*	*2½ cups*

1.   Cook the cauliflower in boiling water until just tender.
2.   Meanwhile, melt the margarine in a frying pan (skillet) and sauté the onion until soft.
3.   Mix together the breadcrumbs, oats, nuts, cheese, herbs and tomato purée, then add the onion in the margarine and mix well.
4.   Press the nut mixture into the base of a large ovenproof dish.

5.   For the white sauce, melt the margarine in a saucepan. Stir in the flour and cook for 2 minutes. Remove from the heat and gradually add the milk. Heat gently, stirring constantly, until thickened.
6.   Drain the cauliflower florets and arrange over the nut base. Pour over the sauce. Bake in a preheated oven at 190°C/375°F/Gas Mark 5 for 10–15 minutes. Serve at once.

Did you know?
Cauliflowers were originally cultivated by the Minoans.

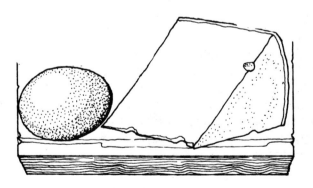

sweet swede flan

Serves 4-6

Ingredients	Metric	Imperial	American
Plain (all-purpose) wholewheat flour	225 g	8 oz	2 cups
Baking powder	2 tsp	2 tsp	2 tsp
Vegetable margarine	100 g	4 oz	½ cup
Yeast extract	½ tsp	½ tsp	½ tsp
Vegetable oil for frying			
Onion, sliced	1 large	1 large	1 large
Swede, cooked and mashed	175 g	6 oz	1½ cups
Free-range eggs	3	3	3
Skimmed milk or soya milk	150 ml	¼ pint	⅔ cup
Grated nutmeg	½ tsp	½ tsp	½ tsp
Cheddar cheese, grated	175 g	6 oz	1½ cups
Large tomatoes, sliced	4	4	4

1. Place the flour and baking powder in a bowl and rub (cut) in the margarine until the mixture resembles breadcrumbs.
2. Dissolve the yeast extract in 4 tbsp water and use to bind the pastry. Mix to a dough, then leave in a cool place for 30 minutes.
3. Meanwhile, heat a little oil in a frying pan (skillet) and sauté the onion for about 5 minutes or until soft. Leave to cool.

4. Roll out the pastry on a lightly floured surface and use to line one 20 cm/8 inch flan ring. Spoon the onion evenly over the base and then add a layer of mashed swede.

5. Beat the eggs, milk and nutmeg together and stir in the cheese. Pour this over the swede and top with tomato slices.

6. Bake in a preheated oven at 190°C/375°F/Gas Mark 5 for 40 minutes, or until golden brown.

Did you know?
Fried onions contain 10% natural sugars.

mung bean cottage pie

Serves 4-6

Ingredients	Metric	Imperial	American
Potatoes, unpeeled	1 kg	2 lb	2 lb
Vegetable margarine	25 g	1 oz	2 tbsp
Skimmed milk or soya milk	3 tbsp	3 tbsp	3 tbsp
Sunflower oil	2 tbsp	2 tbsp	2 tbsp
Chopped onion	1 large	1 large	1 large
Carrots, diced	2	2	2
Celery stalks, diced	2	2	2
Yeast extract	1 tsp	1 tsp	1 tsp
Chopped fresh parsley	25 g	1 oz	1 cup
Dried thyme	pinch	pinch	pinch
Canned tomatoes	400 g	14 oz	3½ cups
Tomato purée (paste)	1 tbsp	1 tbsp	1 tbsp
Cooked mung beans	175 g	6 oz	1 cup
Tomatoes, sliced	2 large	2 large	2 large

1. Cook the potatoes in boiling water until tender. Drain, peel the potatoes and mash with the margarine and milk. (If you own a food processor it is possible to mash the potatoes in their skins, thereby retaining even more goodness.)

2. Heat the sunflower oil in a frying pan (skillet) and sauté the onion, carrot and celery for 5 minutes, stirring constantly.

3. Add the yeast extract, herbs, canned tomatoes with their juice, tomato purée and beans and simmer gently until the vegetables are tender and the liquid reduced.

4. Spoon the vegetable mixture into an ovenproof dish. Spread the mashed potato over the top and decorate using a fork and the tomato slices.

5. Bake in a preheated oven at 190°C/375°F/Gas Mark 5 for 20–30 minutes, or until browned.

Did you know?
Mung beans are the sprouted beans served as Chinese beansprouts in Chinese restaurants. They contain just as much protein as meat.

pancake parcels

Serves 3

Ingredients	Metric	Imperial	American
Plain yoghurt	*2 tbsp*	*2 tbsp*	*2 tbsp*
Skimmed milk or			
soya milk			
Wholewheat flour	*100 g*	*4 oz*	*1 cup*
Free-range eggs, beaten	*2*	*2*	*2*
Yeast extract	*½ tsp*	*½ tsp*	*½ tsp*
Canned baked beans	*6 tbsp*	*6 tbsp*	*6 tbsp*
Vegetable oil for frying			
Grated carrot	*1*	*1*	*1*

1.   Place the yoghurt in a measuring jug and make up to 300 ml/½ pint/1¼ cups with milk.

2.   Place the flour in a large bowl, make a well in the centre and stir in the eggs. Gradually beat in the milk and yoghurt mixture and continue beating until you have a smooth batter. Set aside in a cool place for at least 30 minutes.

3.   Meanwhile, grease three small square ovenproof dishes. Stir the yeast extract into the beans.

4.   Place a little oil in the base of a small frying pan (skillet) and heat. When really hot, pour in a little of the pancake mixture. When this bubbles and begins to set, flip the pancake over and cook for a further 2-3 minutes. (Do not become despondent if the first pancake is a failure as the pan often needs time to heat through.)

5.   Continue making pancakes in this way until all the batter is used and you have six pancakes.

6.   Use two pancakes to line each ovenproof dish. Place a little grated carrot in the base of each, then fill with 2 tbsp beans.

7.   Fold over the pancakes to form parcels. Place the dishes in a baking tin (pan) containing 2.5 cm/ 1 inch water and cook in a preheated oven at 200°C/ 400°F/Gas Mark 6 for 35–40 minutes.

8.   When the pancake parcels are cooked, remove them from the baking tin, unmould onto a hot plate and garnish as liked.

Did you know?
Many processed beans contain sugar so try, if possible, to use a sugar-free variety.

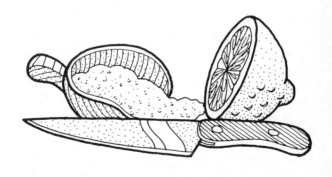

paupers' potato bake

Serves 4

Ingredients	Metric	Imperial	American
Potatoes, washed and cubed	1 kg	2 lb	2 lb
Onions, chopped	2	2	2
Wholewheat flour	50 g	2 oz	½ cup
Chopped fresh parsley	1 tbsp	1 tbsp	1 tbsp
Mixed fresh vegetables (chopped cabbage, peas, carrots, etc.)	175 g	6 oz	1½ cups
Skimmed milk or soya milk	450 ml	¾ pint	2 cups
Plain yoghurt	150 g	5 oz	5 oz
Paprika, to garnish			

1. Mix together the potatoes and onions. Stir in the flour, parsley and cheese.
2. Place half the potato mixture in the bottom of a greased ovenproof dish. Add a layer of mixed vegetables and cover with the remaining potato.
3. Place the milk and yoghurt together in a saucepan and heat until just warm. Pour over the potatoes and vegetables.
4. Bake in a preheated oven at 200°C/400°F/Gas Mark 6 for 1–1½ hours, or until the potatoes are tender.
5. Sprinkle with a little paprika and serve with the salad of your choice.

Did you know?
Cottage cheese contains a quarter of the calories and one twentieth of the fat contained in Cheddar, but it is three times higher in protein.

lentil burgers

These are a much more delicious alternative to greasy meat burgers.

Makes 6

Ingredients	Metric	Imperial	American
Vegetable oil for frying			
Chopped onion	*½*	*½*	*½*
Cooked greeen lentils	*100 g*	*4 oz*	*½ cup*
Cooked peas	*50 g*	*2 oz*	*⅓ cup*
Grated carrot	*1*	*1*	*1*
Chopped fresh parsley	*1 tbsp*	*1 tbsp*	*1 tbsp*
Tamari	*1 tsp*	*1 tsp*	*1 tsp*
Wholewheat breadcrumbs	*100 g*	*4 oz*	*2 cups*
Wholewheat flour	*25 g*	*1 oz*	*¼ cup*
Free-range egg, beaten	*1*	*1*	*1*

1. Heat a little vegetable oil in a frying pan (skillet) and sauté the onion for about 5 minutes, or until soft.

2. Mix all the ingredients, except the flour, together in a large bowl, adding sufficient beaten egg to bind the mixture. Leave to cool.

3. When cold, form the mixture into burger shapes and dust with flour. Fry the burgers in vegetable oil until evenly browned. Serve hot in wholewheat rolls with lots of fresh salad.

Did you know?
The Roman legions depended largely on lentils for their protein.

oodles of noodles

Serves 4

Ingredients

Ingredients	Metric	Imperial	American
Sunflower oil	*2 tbsp*	*2 tbsp*	*2 tbsp*
Wholewheat tagliatelle	*225 g*	*8 oz*	*2 cups*
Chopped onion	*1*	*1*	*1*
Mushrooms, sliced	*100 g*	*4 oz*	*1 cup*
Dried oregano	*1 tsp*	*1 tsp*	*1 tsp*
Dried basil	*1 tsp*	*1 tsp*	*1 tsp*
Canned tomatoes	*400 g*	*14 oz*	*3½ cups*
Tomato purée (paste)	*2 tbsp*	*2 tbsp*	*2 tbsp*
Flaked (slivered) almonds	*50 g*	*2 oz*	*½ cup*
Chopped fresh parsley or chives to garnish			

1. Bring a large saucepan of water to the boil and add a little oil to prevent sticking. Add the tagliatelle and boil vigorously for 8–10 minutes, or until tender, but with some 'bite'.

2. Meanwhile, heat 1 tbsp oil in a frying pan (skillet) and sauté the onion until transparent. Add the mushrooms and herbs and cook for a further 2 minutes.

3. Stir in the tomatoes and tomato purée and simmer gently for 10–15 minutes. (If the sauce becomes too thick, dilute with a little hot vegetable stock or water.) Add the almonds and heat through.

4. Drain the pasta thoroughly, transfer to heated serving plates and pour over the sauce. Garnish with parsley or chives and serve immediately.

Did you know?
The finest pasta is made from durum wheat.

nutty fingers

Serves 4

Ingredients	Metric	Imperial	American
Sunflower oil	*2 tbsp*	*2 tbsp*	*2 tbsp*
Chopped onion	*1*	*1*	*1*
Grated carrot	*1*	*1*	*1*
Ground mixed nuts	*225 g*	*8 oz*	*2 cups*
Rolled oats	*50 g*	*2 oz*	*½ cup*
Soya flour	*25 g*	*1 oz*	*½ cup*
Tomato purée paste	*2 tbsp*	*2 tbsp*	*2 tbsp*
Wholewheat breadcrumbs	*100 g*	*4 oz*	*2 cups*
Yeast extract	*1 tsp*	*1 tsp*	*1 tsp*
Dried mixed herbs	*1 tsp*	*1 tsp*	*1 tsp*
Free-range egg, beaten	*1*	*1*	*1*

1.   Heat the oil in a frying pan (skillet) and sauté the onion until transparent. Stir in the carrot and cook for a further 2 minutes.

2.   In a bowl, combine the nuts, oats, soya flour, tomato purée, breadcrumbs, yeast extract and herbs. Add the carrots and onions with the oil and mix well. Pour in enough beaten egg to form a stiff dough.

3.   Using floured hands, shape the mixture into fingers. Place on a greased baking sheet and brush with a little oil. Bake in a preheated oven at 180°C/350°F/Gas Mark 4 for 15 minutes, or until golden. Serve with tomato sauce and green vegetables.

Did you know?
Peanuts have the highest fat content and chestnuts the lowest.

chinese stir-fry

To turn this dish into something really fun, give everyone a pair of chopsticks and standby for the laughter. It is the most painless way I know to persuade youngsters to eat up their vegetables.

Serves 4

Ingredients	Metric	Imperial	American
Sunflower oil	3 tbsp	3 tbsp	3 tbsp
Chopped onion	1	1	1
Firm tofu, cubed	225 g	8 oz	½ lb
Chopped cabbage	50 g	2 oz	½ cup
Green peas	100 g	4 oz	1 cup
Mushrooms, sliced	50 g	2 oz	½ cup
Tomatoes, chopped	2	2	2
Beansprouts	225 g	8 oz	4 cups
Shoyu or tamari	2 tsp	2 tsp	2 tsp

1. Heat the oil in a wok or large frying pan (skillet) and stir-fry the onion until transparent.
2. Add the tofu to the pan and stir-fry for a further 2 minutes. Stir in the remaining vegetables, except the beansprouts, and stir-fry for a further 3–4 minutes.
3. Finally, stir in the shoyu or tamari and beansprouts and heat through. Serve at once with plenty of brown rice.

Did you know?
Tofu is made from soya beans, is high in protein and contains no cholesterol.

tofu minty pasties

Makes 6

Ingredients	Metric	Imperial	American
Wholewheat flour	225 g	8 oz	2 cups
Baking powder	1 tsp	1 tsp	1 tsp
Vegetable margarine	100 g	4 oz	½ cup
Chopped onion	1	1	1
Tomato, chopped	1	1	1
Cooked green peas	50 g	2 oz	⅓ cup
Cooked potato, diced	100 g	4 oz	⅔ cup
Firm tofu, cubed	100 g	4 oz	¼ lb
Tomato purée (paste)	2 tbsp	2 tbsp	2 tbsp
Chopped fresh mint	1 tbsp	1 tbsp	1 tbsp
Milk to glaze			

1.   Place the flour and baking powder in a bowl, add the margarine and rub (cut) it in until the mixture resembles breadcrumbs. Make a well in the centre and pour in 4 tbsp cold water. Mix to a stiff dough and refrigerate for 30 minutes.
2.   Mix together the vegetables, tofu, tomato purée and mint.
3.   Roll out the pastry on a lightly floured surface and cut into rounds using a saucer as a guide.
4.   Place a large spoonful of the vegetable and tofu mixture on each round of pastry. Moisten the edges with water and gather up to form a pasty.
5.   Brush each pasty with milk. Place on a greased baking tray and bake in a preheated oven at 220°C/425°F/Gas Mark 7 for 30 minutes. Serve with salad or a seasonal vegetable.

Did you know?
The Chinese refer to tofu as the 'meat without a bone'.

macaroni medley

Serves 4-6

Ingredients	Metric	Imperial	American
Wholewheat macaroni	*225 g*	*8 oz*	*2 cups*
Sunflower oil	*1 tbsp*	*1 tbsp*	*1 tbsp*
Chopped onion	*1*	*1*	*1*
Mushrooms, sliced	*100 g*	*4 oz*	*1 cup*
Vegetable margarine	*25 g*	*1 oz*	*2 tbsp*
Wholewheat flour	*25 g*	*1 oz*	*¼ cup*
Skimmed milk or soya milk	*300 ml*	*½ pint*	*1¼ cups*
Cheddar cheese, grated	*175 g*	*6 oz*	*1½ cups*
Chopped walnuts	*50 g*	*2 oz*	*½ cup*

1. Bring a large saucepan of water to the boil and add 1 tsp oil to prevent sticking. Add the macaroni and cook for 12 minutes, or until tender. Drain and set aside.

2. Heat the oil in a frying pan (skillet) and sauté the onion for about 5 minutes, or until softened. Add the mushrooms and cook for 2 minutes. Set aside.

3. Melt the margarine in a saucepan, stir in the flour and cook for 2–3 minutes. Remove from the heat and gradually stir in the milk. Bring to the boil and cook, stirring, until thickened. Add the grated cheese and beat until smooth.

4.   Fold the macaroni and walnuts into the cheese sauce. Place a layer of macaroni in the bottom of an ovenproof dish, then add a layer of mushrooms. Continue in this way, ending with a layer of macaroni. Bake in a preheated oven at 220°C/ 425°F/Gas Mark 7 for 20 minutes, or until brown and bubbling.

Did you know?
Walnuts are the most easily digested of all nuts.

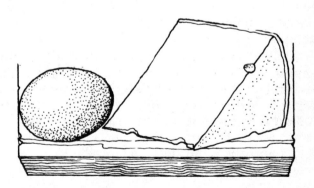

garbanzos and grains

Serves 4

Ingredients	Metric	Imperial	American
Vegetable oil	*2 tbsp*	*2 tbsp*	*2 tbsp*
Chopped onion	*1*	*1*	*1*
Carrots, sliced	*2*	*2*	*2*
Small cauliflower broken into florets	*1*	*1*	*1*
Medium-sized potatoes, washed and diced	*3*	*3*	*3*
Mushrooms, sliced	*100 g*	*4 oz*	*1 cup*
Pot barley	*175 g*	*6 oz*	*1 cup*
Cooked chick-peas	*100 g*	*4 oz*	*⅔ cup*
Vegetable extract	*1 tsp*	*1 tsp*	*1 tsp*
Vegetable stock or water	*600 ml*	*1 pint*	*2½ cups*
Bay leaf	*1*	*1*	*1*
Tamari or shoyu sauce	*1 tsp*	*1 tsp*	*1 tsp*

1. Heat the oil in a large frying pan (skillet) and sauté the onion for about 5 minutes, or until soft.

2. Add the remaining vegetables, barley and chick-peas. Dissolve the vegetable extract in the stock or water and pour into the pan with the bay leaf and sauce. Stir well and leave overnight, or for at least 4–5 hours, to soften the barley and allow the flavours to mingle.

3. Next day, bring the mixture to the boil and simmer gently for about 20 minutes, or until the stock is absorbed and the vegetables tender. Discard the bay leaf.

4. Serve in bowls with crusty wholewheat bread.

Did you know?
Chick-peas are also known as garbanzos and
contain as much protein as steak.

vegetarian goulash

Serves 4

Ingredients	Metric	Imperial	American
Textured vegetable protein (TVP) or soya mince	100 g	4 oz	¼ lb
Sunflower oil	2 tbsp	2 tbsp	2 tbsp
Onion, sliced	1	1	1
Wholewheat flour	25 g	1 oz	¼ cup
Paprika	1 tsp	1 tsp	1 tsp
Vegetable stock	300 ml	½ pint	1¼ cups
Canned tomatoes	400 g	14 oz	3½ cups
Carrots, diced	3	3	3
Courgettes (zucchini), thinly sliced	3	3	3
Potatoes, washed and diced	225 g	8 oz	½ lb
Chopped green (bell) pepper	½	½	½
Diced parsnips	2	2	2
Small cauliflower, broken in florets	1	1	1
Plain yoghurt	150 g	5 oz	5 oz
Freshly ground black pepper			

1. Place the mince in a bowl and pour over sufficient boiling water to hydrate it. Leave to stand for 1 hour.

2.   Heat the oil in a large frying pan (skillet) and sauté the onion for about 5 minutes, or until soft. Stir in the flour and paprika and cook for 1 minute. Stir in the stock. Add the tomatoes and boil. Remove from the heat and stir in all the remaining vegetables.

3.   Drain the mince and add to the pan. Pour the goulash into a large ovenproof casserole, cover and bake in a preheated oven at 180°C/350°F/Gas Mark 5 for 1 hour, or until tender.

4.   Just before serving, stir in the yoghurt and season with black pepper. Garnish with a little extra paprika, if liked.

Did you know?
Soya contains four times more protein than eggs and 12 times more calcium than milk.

lentil cannelloni

Serves 4-6

Ingredients	Metric	Imperial	American
Wholewheat lasagne sheets	12	12	12
Sunflower oil	2 tbsp	2 tbsp	2 tbsp
Chopped onions	2	2	2
Diced carrots	2	2	2
Wholewheat breadcrumbs	50 g	2 oz	1 cup
Cooked red lentils	100 g	4 oz	⅔ cup
Dried basil	1 tsp	1 tsp	1 tsp
Tomato purée (paste)	2 tsp	2 tsp	2 tsp
Chopped fresh parsley	2 tbsp	2 tbsp	2 tbsp
Free-range egg, beaten	1	1	1
Canned tomatoes	400 g	14 oz	3½ cups
Grated Parmesan cheese	2 tbsp	2 tbsp	2 tbsp

1.   Bring a large saucepan of water to the boil, add the lasagne and cook for 8–10 minutes, or until just tender. A little oil added to the water will prevent the lasagne sticking. Drain and set aside.

2.   Heat the oil in a frying pan (skillet) and sauté the onion and carrot for about 5 minutes, or until soft. Drain and place in a large bowl. Add the breadcrumbs, lentils, basil, tomato purée and parsley, and enough beaten egg to bind the mixture together.

3. Lay the lasagne out and spread each sheet with some of the mixture. Roll up and place in a greased ovenproof dish.

4. Liquidize the tomatoes in a blender or food processor and pour over the cannelloni. Sprinkle with Parmesan and bake in a preheated oven at 200°C/400°F/Gas Mark 6 for 30 minutes. Serve with a mixed salad.

Did you know?
The lens was named after the lentil because of its shape.

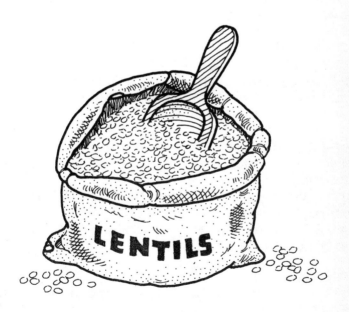

burnham baked beans

A home-made alternative to the canned variety.

Serves 4

Ingredients	Metric	Imperial	American
Haricot (navy) beans	*225 g*	*8 oz*	*1 cup*
Sunflower oil	*1 tbsp*	*1 tbsp*	*1 tbsp*
Chopped onion	*1 large*	*1 large*	*1 large*
Canned tomatoes	*400 g*	*14 oz*	*3½ cups*
Molasses	*1 tbsp*	*1 tbsp*	*1 tbsp*
Brown sugar	*1 tsp*	*1 tsp*	*1 tsp*
Dried mixed herbs	*pinch*	*pinch*	*pinch*
Mustard powder	*1 tsp*	*1 tsp*	*1 tsp*
Tomato purée (paste)	*1 tbsp*	*1 tbsp*	*1 tbsp*

1.   Soak the beans in cold water overnight, drain, then cook in boiling water until soft. Drain again.

2.   Heat the oil in a frying pan (skillet) and sauté the onion for about 5 minutes, or until soft. Add the beans and tomatoes to the onion, stirring well.

3.   Mix together the molasses, sugar, herbs, mustard and tomato purée. Add sufficient water to give a thick sauce. Pour onto the beans and place in a large casserole.

4.   Cook in a preheated oven at 160°/325°F/Gas Mark 3 for at least 3 hours. Stir occasionally to prevent sticking. The longer you allow the beans to cook the better the flavour.

Did you know?
There are over 1,000 different varities of beans and lentils.

rosy risotto

Serves 4

Ingredients	Metric	Imperial	American
Sunflower oil	3 tbsp	3 tbsp	3 tbsp
Onions, sliced	2	2	2
Beansprouts	100 g	4 oz	2 cups
Cooked long-grain brown rice	225 g	8 oz	1½ cups
Canned baked beans	2 tbsp	2 tbsp	2 tbsp
Tomato purée (paste)	1 tbsp	1 tbsp	1 tbsp

1. Heat the oil in a frying pan (skillet) and sauté the onion for about 5 minutes, or until soft. Add the beansprouts and rice and stir-fry until heated through.
2. Stir in the beans and tomato purée, adding a little water if the mixture appears too dry. Continue to stir-fry until the risotto is well mixed and hot.
3. Serve with a large salad.

Did you know?
The nutritional value of some beans increases by up to 600% when the beans are sprouted.

crumbly corn and tomato

Serves 4

Ingredients	Metric	Imperial	American
Sunflower oil	2 tbsp	2 tbsp	2 tbsp
Chopped onions	2	2	2
Medium-size courgettes (zucchini), sliced	4	4	4
Tomatoes, roughly chopped	6	6	6
Sweetcorn (whole kernel corn)	100 g	4 oz	¾ cup
Tomato purée (paste)	2 tbsp	2 tbsp	2 tbsp
Tamaari or soya sauce	1 tsp	1 tsp	1 tsp
Crumble			
Rolled oats	50 g	2 oz	½ cup
Wholewheat breadcrumbs	175 g	6 oz	3 cups
Vegetable margarine	75 g	3 oz	⅓ cup
Sunflower seeds	50 g	2 oz	½ cup

1. Heat the oil in a large frying pan (skillet) or wok and sauté the onion for about 5 minutes, or until soft. Add the courgettes and stir-fry until tender. Stir in the tomatoes and sweetcorn and stir-fry for a further 3–4 minutes.

2. Mix the tomato purée with the tamari or soya sauce and a little water to give a pouring consistency. Stir this into the vegetables. Simmer gently for 5 minutes.

3.   Place the oats and breadcrumbs in a bowl, add the margarine and rub (cut) it in. Stir in the sunflower seeds.

4.   Put the vegetable mixture in a deep casserole and spoon over the crumble. Bake in a preheated oven at 190°C/375°F/Gas Mark 5 for 20 minutes, or until just beginning to brown.

Did you know?
Sunflower seeds are 15% protein.

black-eyed susies' casserole

Serves 4

Ingredients	Metric	Imperial	American
Vegetable oil	*3 tbsp*	*3 tbsp*	*3 tbsp*
Onion, sliced	*1*	*1*	*1*
Carrots, sliced	*2*	*2*	*2*
Small cauliflower,			
broken into florets	*1*	*1*	*1*
Vegetable extract	*1 tsp*	*1 tsp*	*1 tsp*
Vegetable stock or water	*300 ml*	*½ pint*	*1¼ cups*
Tomato purée (paste)	*4 tbsp*	*4 tbsp*	*4 tbsp*
Canned tomatoes	*400 g*	*14 oz*	*3½ cups*
Cooked black-eyed beans	*350 g*	*12 oz*	*2 cups*
Chopped fresh parsley	*2 tbsp*	*2 tbsp*	*2 tbsp*
Cheddar cheese, grated	*100 g*	*4 oz*	*1 cup*

1.   Heat the oil in a large pan and sauté the onion for about 5 minutes, or until soft and transparent. Add the carrots and cauliflower and stir-fry for 4–5 minutes.

2.   In a small bowl, blend the vegetable extract into the stock or water and stir in the tomato purée. Pour onto the pan of vegetables, stirring gently. Add the tomatoes, beans and parsley. Simmer for about 5 minutes, or until the vegetables are just tender, adding more stock if necessary. Transfer to a heated serving dish.

3.   Sprinkle with grated cheese and serve.

Did you know?
Soldiers christened black-eyed beans 'Susies' during the war when they formed a major part of their diet.

roman sausages

Serves 4

Ingredients	Metric	Imperial	American
Wholewheat breadcrumbs	75 g	3 oz	1½ cups
Cheddar cheese, grated	40 g	1½ oz	6 tbsp
Pine nuts	25 g	1 oz	¼ cup
Dried mixed herbs	½ tsp	½ tsp	½ tsp
Chopped onion	1 tsp	1 tsp	1 tsp
Chopped tomato	1	1	1
Free-range egg, separated	1 small	1 small	1 small
Wholewheat flour	25 g	1 oz	¼ cup
Wholewheat breadcrumbs	2 tbsp	2 tbsp	2 tbsp
Vegetable oil	2 tbsp	2 tbsp	2 tbsp

1. In a large bowl, mix together the breadcrumbs, cheese, nuts, herbs, onion and tomato. Add enough egg yolk to bind the mixture.
2. Shape the mixture into small sausages and roll in the flour. Brush with a little beaten egg white and finally coat with the breadcrumbs.
3. Heat the oil in a frying pan (skillet) and sauté the sausages until golden brown. Serve immediately with a tomato sauce.

Did you know?
Sausages were mentioned in the oldest cookery book, in AD228. The Romans' favourite recipe included pine nuts.

vegetable and nut bake

Serves 4

Ingredients	Metric	Imperial	American
Vegetable margarine	*50 g*	*2 oz*	*¼ cup*
Wholewheat flour	*25 g*	*1 oz*	*¼ cup*
Skimmed milk or			
soya milk	*300 ml*	*½ pint*	*1¼ cups*
Cooked chopped			
cabbage	*100 g*	*4 oz*	*⅔ cup*
Cooked green peas	*100 g*	*4 oz*	*⅔ cup*
Cooked carrots, sliced	*100 g*	*4 oz*	*⅔ cup*
Sultanas (golden raisins)	*25 g*	*1 oz*	*¼ cup*
Wholewheat breadcrumbs	*3 tbsp*	*3 tbsp*	*3 tbsp*
Sliced mushrooms	*50 g*	*2 oz*	*½ cup*
Base			
Wholewheat breadcrumbs	*175 g*	*6 oz*	*3 cups*
Vegetable margarine	*50 g*	*2 oz*	*¼ cup*
Chopped mixed nuts	*75 g*	*3 oz*	*¾ cup*
Cheddar cheese, grated	*75 g*	*3 oz*	*¾ cup*
Chopped onion	*1*	*1*	*1*
Tomato purée (paste)	*1 tbsp*	*1 tbsp*	*1 tbsp*

1. For the base, place the breadcrumbs in a large bowl, add the margarine and rub (cut) in. Stir in the nuts, cheese, onion and tomato purée. Press the mixture into the base of a medium-size casserole. Bake in a preheated oven at 220°C/425°F/Gas Mark 7 for 15 minutes. Reduce the oven temperature to 190°C/375°F/Gas Mark 5.

2. For the sauce, heat the margarine and blend in the flour. Cook for 2 minutes, then remove from the heat and gradually stir in the milk. Bring to the boil and cook, stirring, until thickened.

3. Add the vegetables and sultanas and pour over the nut base. Sprinkle with breadcrumbs and decorate with the mushrooms. Bake in the oven for 15 minutes, or until bubbling and browned.

Did you know?
Other than coconuts, the fat in all nuts is unsaturated.

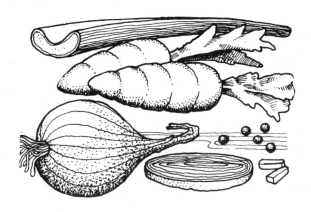

hummus

Serves 6

Ingredients	Metric	Imperial	American
Cooked chick-peas	*225 g*	*8 oz*	*1⅓ cups*
Tahini	*50 g*	*2 oz*	*2 oz*
Garlic cloves, crushed	*2*	*2*	*2*
Lemon juice	*4 tbsp*	*4 tbsp*	*4 tbsp*
Olive oil	*3 tbsp*	*3 tbsp*	*3 tbsp*
Freshly ground black pepper			

1. Place all the ingredients in a blender or food processor and blend until smooth. The consistency should be fairly soft. If it is a little too stiff, add extra water to thin.

2. Serve as a dip surrounded with a colourful mixture of salad vegetables, or as a sandwich spread.

Did you know?
Chick-peas contain more calcium than cows' milk. Tahini is a paste made from toasted sesame seeds.

urchins' omelette

Serves 2

Ingredients	Metric	Imperial	American
Soya flour	1 tsp	1 tsp	1 tsp
Skimmed milk or soya milk	2 tbsp	2 tbsp	2 tbsp
Free-range eggs, lightly beaten	3	3	3
Sunflower oil for frying			
Chopped onion	1 tbsp	1 tbsp	1 tbsp
Cooked medium-size potato, diced	1	1	1
Cooked diced carrot	2 tbsp	2 tbsp	2 tbsp
Cooked peas	2 tbsp	2 tbsp	2 tbsp

1. In a small bowl, blend the soya flour into the milk and beat it into the eggs.

2. Heat a little oil in a small frying pan (skillet) and sauté the onion for about 5 minutes, or until transparent. Add the remaining vegetables and stir-fry for 2–3 minutes, or until heated through.

3. Pour the egg mixture onto the vegetables and cook gently until the egg has set.

4. Turn the omelette onto a warmed serving plate and cut into two portions if necessary. Serve with tomato sauce and green beans.

Did you know?
The cholesterol content of eggs lies in the yolks.

swede and potato pie

Serves 4

Ingredients	Metric	Imperial	American
Medium-size swede (rutabaga), diced	1	1	1
Potatoes, unpeeled and diced	750 g	1½ lb	1½ lb
Vegetable margarine	25 g	1 oz	2 tbsp
Dried thyme	pinch	pinch	pinch
Vegetable oil	1 tbsp	1 tbsp	1 tbsp
Chopped onion	1	1	1
Mushrooms, sliced	2-3	2-3	2-3
Canned baked beans, drained	450 g	1 lb	1 lb
Tomatoes, sliced	2-3	2-3	2-3

1. Place the swede in a saucepan with the potatoes and cover with water. Bring to the boil and cook for 15–20 minutes, or until tender. Drain and mash by hand or in a food processor. Beat in the margarine and set aside.
2. Heat the oil in a frying pan (skillet) and sauté the chopped onion for about 5 minutes, or until transparent. Add the mushrooms and stir-fry for 2–3 minutes. Stir in the baked beans.
3. Place half the potato mixture in the base of a large casserole. Spoon in the bean mixture and cover with the remaining potato. Arrange tomato slices on top and bake in a preheated oven at 190°C/375°F/Gas Mark 5 for 30 minutes, or until golden.

Did you know?
Grated raw swede is just as delicious as grated carrot.

oriental beansprouts

Serves 2

Ingredients	Metric	Imperial	American
Beansprouts	*225 g*	*8 oz*	*4 cups*
Sliced spring onions			
(scallions)	*1 tbsp*	*1 tbsp*	*1 tbsp*
Diced red (bell) pepper	*½*	*½*	*½*
Sliced mushrooms	*50-75 g*	*2-3 oz*	*½-¾ cup*
Dressing			
Plain yoghurt	*150 g*	*5 oz*	*5 oz*
Lemon juice	*1 tbsp*	*1 tbsp*	*1 tbsp*
Garlic clove, crushed			
(optional)	*1 small*	*1 small*	*1 small*
Low-fat mayonnaise	*1 tbsp*	*1 tbsp*	*1 tbsp*
Tamari or shoyu	*1 tsp*	*1 tsp*	*1 tsp*
Grated fresh root ginger	*1 tsp*	*1 tsp*	*1 tsp*

1. Place the beansprouts in a salad bowl, add all the other vegetables and mix well.
2. To make the dressing, place the ingredients in a jug and whisk well to combine. Alternatively, use a screw-top jar and shake well.
3. Pour the dressing over the salad, toss and chill thoroughly before serving.

Did you know?
25 g/1 oz/½ cup beansprouts contains the equivalent amount of vitamin C to 6 glasses of orange juice?

cabbage roll-mops

This is a wonderful way to encourage youngsters to eat cabbage and it's a world away from the soggy cabbage of school dinners.

Serves 4

Ingredients	Metric	Imperial	American
Sunflower oil	2 tbsp	2 tbsp	2 tbsp
Onions, finely chopped	2	2	2
Finely chopped celery stalk	1	1	1
Tomatoes, chopped	4	4	4
Cooked long-grain brown rice	100 g	4 oz	¾ cup
Dried basil	2 tsp	2 tsp	2 tsp
Raisins	50 g	2 oz	⅓ cup
Flaked (slivered) almonds	50 g	2 oz	½ cup
Tomato purée (paste)	4 tbsp	4 tbsp	4 tbsp
Even-sized cabbage leaves	8	8	8
Water	200 ml	⅓ pint	⅞ cup

1. Heat the oil in a large frying pan (skillet) or wok and sauté the onion for about 5 minutes, or until soft. Stir in the celery and tomatoes and cook for a further 3–4 minutes, stirring constantly. Add the rice, basil, raisins, almonds and 1 tbsp tomato purée, and mix well.

2.   Lay the cabbage leaves out on a board and remove the thick central veins. Fill each leaf with a portion of the rice mixture. Fold over the sides and roll up.

3.   Place the cabbage parcels in a greased ovenproof dish. Dilute the remaining tomato purée with the water and pour around the cabbage. Cover and bake for 35 minutes in a preheated oven at 180°C/350°F/Gas Mark 4. Serve with roast potatoes and vegetables.

Did you know?
Almonds are higher in protein than other nuts.

continental lentil lasagne

Serves 4

Ingredients	Metric	Imperial	American
Pre-cooked wholewheat lasagne sheets	12	12	12
Sunflower oil	2 tbsp	2 tbsp	2 tbsp
Chopped onions	2	2	2
Garlic clove, crushed	1	1	1
Carrots, finely chopped	2	2	2
Celery stalks, finely chopped	2	2	2
Canned tomatoes	400 g	14 oz	3½ cups
Tomato purée (paste)	4 tbsp	4 tbsp	4 tbsp
Cooked continental (green) lentils	175 g	6 oz	1 cup
Dried oregano	1 tsp	1 tsp	1 tsp
Dried basil	1 tsp	1 tsp	1 tsp
Vegetable extract	1 tsp	1 tsp	1 tsp
Wholewheat breadcrumbs	2 tbsp	2 tbsp	2 tbsp
Cheese sauce			
Vegetable margarine	50 g	2 oz	¼ cup
Wholewheat flour	50 g	2 oz	½ cup
Skimmed milk or soya milk	600 ml	1 pint	2½ cups
Cheddar cheese, grated	100 g	4 oz	1 cup

1. Lightly grease a 23 cm/9 inch square oven-proof dish. Place 4 sheets of lasagne in the bottom of the dish.

2.   Heat the sunflower oil in a large saucepan and lightly sauté the onion and garlic. Add the carrots and celery and stir-fry for about 5 minutes, or until tender. Stir in the canned tomatoes, tomato purée, lentils and herbs and simmer gently.

3.   Blend the vegetable extract with a little hot water and add to the pan. Simmer for 15 minutes, stirring occasionally.

4.   Meanwhile, make the cheese sauce. Melt the margarine in a saucepan and stir in the flour. Cook for 2 minutes, then remove from the heat and gradually add the milk. Bring to the boil and cook, stirring, until thickened and smooth. Stir in the cheese until melted and remove from the heat.

5.   Assemble the lasagne by pouring a layuer of the vegetable mixture over the pasta. Follow with another layer of pasta, then vegetables and finally pasta. Pour over the cheese sauce, sprinkle with the breadcrumbs and bake in a preheated oven at 190°C/375°F/Gas Mark 5 for 30 minutes. Serve with salad.

Did you know?
Canned tomatoes contain 50% more iron than fresh, but 50% less calcium.

three-bean salad

Serves 4

Ingredients	Metric	Imperial	American
Cooked red kidney beans	100 g	4 oz	⅓ cup
Cooked chick-peas	100 g	4 oz	⅔ cup
Cooked haricot (navy) beans	100 g	4 oz	⅓ cup
Eating apple, cored and diced	1	1	1
Celery stalk, diced	1	1	1
Chopped onion	1	1	1
Dressing			
Sunflower oil	120 ml	4 fl oz	½ cup
Cider vinegar	2 tbsp	2 tbsp	2 tbsp
Apple juice concentrate	1 tbsp	1 tbsp	1 tbsp
Lemon juice	1 tsp	1 tsp	1 tsp

1. In a large bowl, mix together the beans, apple, celery and onion.
2. To make the dressing, place the sunflower oil in a bowl and beat in the vinegar, apple and lemon juices.
3. Pour the dressing over the beans, toss well and refrigerate for several hours before serving with plenty of crusty wholewheat bread.

Did you know?
Haricot beans were the original beans eaten by cowboys in the American 'wild west'.

yellow mint bricks

These make a pleasant alternative to potatoes.

Serves 4

Ingredients	Metric	Imperial	American
Water	*600 ml*	*1 pint*	*2½ cups*
Vegetable margarine	*25 g*	*1 oz*	*2 tbsp*
Cornmeal (Polenta)	*100 g*	*4 oz*	*1 cup*
Chopped onion	*1 small*	*1 small*	*1 small*
Chopped fresh mint	*1 tbsp*	*1 tbsp*	*1 tbsp*
Free-range egg, beaten	*1*	*1*	*1*
Extra cornmeal (polenta), to coat			
Vegetable oil for deep frying			

1. Pour the water into a large saucepan, add the margarine and bring to the boil. Slowly sprinkle in the cornmeal and stir in the onion. Cook slowly, stirring frequently, for about 20 minutes, or until a thick porridge forms. Remove from the heat and stir in the mint.
2. Spoon the cornmeal mixture into a greased 15 cm/6 inch square dish and leave to cool.
3. When the polenta is cold, cut into bricks and coat with beaten egg, then extra cornmeal.
4. Heat the oil in a deep frying pan. To make sure the oil is hot enough, drop a small piece of potato into the oil. When it sizzles, the oil is ready. Deep-fry the polenta bricks for 3–4 minutes, or until golden brown.
5. Drain the bricks well and serve with tomato sauce.

CHAPTER 8

sweet SURPRISES

i have included this section for those who find the prospect of total sugar abstinence too much of a culture shock. The recipes, however, have been devised using comparatively low levels of sugar and including other more wholesome ingredients. With the passing of time and, hopefully, the sweet tooth, you may be able to reduce the sugar still further or replace it with apple juice concentrate.

Use these recipes whenever you feel a piece of fruit just won't do, or to help in the weaning-off-sugar process. Encourage youngsters to enjoy home-made wholewheat cakes and puddings instead of store-bought, sugar-laden products. You will still have some way to go, but you will have taken a major step in the right direction.

cherry and oat cheesecake

Serves 8

Ingredients	Metric	Imperial	American
Vegetable margarine	*100 g*	*4 oz*	*½ cup*
Dark (blackstrap) molasses	*1 tbsp*	*1 tbsp*	*1 tbsp*
Mild honey			
(e.g. heather honey)	*2 tbsp*	*2 tbsp*	*2 tbsp*
Rolled oats	*225 g*	*8 oz*	*2 cups*
Free-range eggs, separated	*3*	*3*	*3*
Fromage blanc or			
ricotta cheese	*450 g*	*1 lb*	*1 lb*
Redcurrant jelly	*1 tbsp*	*1 tbsp*	*1 tbsp*
Ripe cherries, stoned			
(pitted)	*225 g*	*8 oz*	*½ lb*

1.   Melt the margarine, molasses and 1 tbsp honey in a saucepan and stir in the oats. Pour into the bottom of a 23 cm/9 inch loose-bottomed cake tin (springform pan) and bake in a preheated oven at 190°C/375°F/Gas Mark 5 for 15 minutes.
2.   Beat the egg yolks and stir into the cheese. Beat in the remaining honey and the redcurrant jelly, then stir in the cherries, reserving 12 for decoration.
3.   Whisk the egg whites until stiff and fold into the mixture. Pour on top of the oat base and bake at 190°C/375°F/Gas Mark 5 for 20 minutes.
4.   Allow to cool in the tin and, when cold, remove from the tin and decorate with the reserved cherries.

Did you know?
Molasses is the most unrefined of all the sugars and the richest in minerals.

orange and grapefruit baskets

Serves 4

Ingredients	Metric	Imperial	American
Large juicy grapefruit	*1*	*1*	*1*
Large juicy oranges	*4*	*4*	*4*
Apple juice concentrate	*1 tbsp*	*1 tbsp*	*1 tbsp*
Free-range egg whites	*2*	*2*	*2*
Brown sugar	*50 g*	*2 oz*	*⅓ cup*
Flaked (slivered) almonds	*25 g*	*1 oz*	*¼ cup*

1. Cut the grapefruit in half and remove the flesh. Cut a 'cap' off each orange and remove the flesh. Reserve the 'caps'. Cut the flesh of both fruits in bite-sized pieces and place in a bowl with the apple juice concentrate. Stir to mix.

2. Trim a little from the base of each orange peel shell so that they stand upright. Stand in an ovenproof dish and fill each shell with fruit.

3. Whisk the egg whites until stiff and fold in the sugar. Pile on top of each orange and sprinkle with the almonds.

4. Brown in a preheated oven at 190°C/375°F/ Gas Mark 5 for 10 minutes.

5. Cut four strips from the reserved orange caps to form handles for the orange baskets. Serve warm.

Did you know?
An orange contains a day's supply of vitamin C.

peanut flan

Serves 4

Ingredients	Metric	Imperial	American
Plain (all-purpose) wholewheat flour	200 g	7 oz	1¾ cups
Baking powder	2 tsp	2 tsp	2 tsp
Vegetable margarine	90 g	3½ oz	7 tbsp
Ice-cold water	3 tbsp	3 tbsp	3 tbsp
Cornflour (cornstarch)	3 tbsp	3 tbsp	3 tbsp
Brown sugar	100 g	4 oz	⅔ cup
Skimmed milk or soya milk	600 ml	1 pint	2½ pints
Crunchy peanut butter	100 g	4 oz	¼ lb
Free-range eggs, beaten	2	2	2
Unsalted peanuts	100 g	4 oz	½ cup

1. Place the flour and baking powder in a bowl and rub (cut) in the margarine until the mixture resembles breadcrumbs. Make a well in the centre, add the water and mix to a dough. Cover and chill for at least 30 minutes.

2. Roll out the pastry on a lightly floured surface and use to line a 20 cm/8 inch flan tin (pie pan) or ring placed on a baking sheet.

3. Mix the cornflour and sugar. Add a little of the milk and mix to a smooth paste. Heat the remaining milk and pour in the paste, stirring continuously.

4.   Pour a little of the milk onto the peanut butter and blend. When completely blended, pour back into the pan and simmer, stirring, until thickened. Quickly pour the milk over the beaten eggs and return to the saucepan. Cook for a further 2 minutes. Stir in the peanuts and pour into the flan. Bake in a preheated oven at 190°C/375°F/Gas Mark 5 for 10–15 minutes. Serve warm.

Did you know?
Very young children (up to the age of about five) should not be given whole nuts in case they stick in their throats.

pink and green walnut meringues

Serves 4

Ingredients	Metric	Imperial	American
Free-range egg whites	2	2	2
Brown sugar	50 g	2 oz	⅓ cup
Chopped walnuts	25 g	1 oz	¼ cup
Natural red food colouring	1 drop	1 drop	1 drop
Natural green food colouring	1 drop	1 drop	1 drop
Plain Greek-style yoghurt	225 g	8 oz	½ lb
Mild honey (e.g. heather honey)	1 tbsp	1 tbsp	1 tbsp

1.   Whisk the eggs whites until very stiff. Fold in the sugar and nuts using a metal spoon.

2.   Divide the meringue into two portions and quickly stir in the colourings. Drop spoonfuls of the meringue onto greased greaseproof (waxed) paper on baking trays. Bake very slowly in a preheated oven at 120°C/250°F/Gas Mark ½ until thoroughly dried out. If the meringues begin to brown, leave the oven door open for a time. Leave to cool.

3.   Mix together the yoghurt and honey and use to sandwich the meringues together. Serve with fresh fruit.

Did you know?
Most commercial food colourings are chemicals. Healthfood shops sell food colourings which are extracted from natural sources.

grape tart

Serves 2

Ingredients	Metric	Imperial	American
Plain (all-purpose)			
* wholewheat flour*	*175 g*	*6 oz*	*1½ cups*
Ground almonds	*25 g*	*1 oz*	*¼ cup*
Baking powder	*2 tsp*	*2 tsp*	*2 tsp*
Vegetable margarine	*90 g*	*3½ oz*	*7 tbsp*
Ice-cold water	*3 tbsp*	*3 tbsp*	*3 tbsp*
Apple juice	*300 ml*	*½ pint*	*1¼ cups*
Agar-agar	*1 tsp*	*1 tsp*	*1 tsp*
Seedless grapes	*450 g*	*1 lb*	*1 lb*

1.   Place the flour, ground almonds and baking powder in a bowl and rub (cut) in the margarine until the mixture resembles breadcrumbs. Make a well in the centre, add the water and mix to a smooth dough. Cover and chill for at least 30 minutes.

2.   Roll out the pastry on a lightly floured surface and use to line a 23 cm/9 inch flan (pie) dish. Bake blind in a preheated oven at 220°C/425°F/ Gas Mark 7 for 10–15 minutes. Leave to cool.

3.   Gently heat the apple juice in a saucepan and stir in the agar-agar. Bring to the boil and set aside to cool slightly.

4.   Arrange the grapes in the base of the flan. Pour over the jelly and chill until set before serving.

Did you know?
Fresh grapes contain 20 milligrams of vitamin C per 450 g/1 lb, but dried grapes (currants, sultanas and raisins) contain none.

apple crumble flan

Serves 6-8

Ingredients	Metric	Imperial	American
Pastry			
Plain (all-purpose)			
wholewheat flour	*200 g*	*7 oz*	*1¾ cups*
Baking powder	*2 tsp*	*2 tsp*	*2 tsp*
Vegetable margarine	*90 g*	*3½ oz*	*7 tbsp*
Ice-cold water	*3 tbsp*	*3 tbsp*	*3 tbsp*
Filling			
Large cooking (tart)			
apples	*2*	*2*	*2*
Lemon juice	*1 tbsp*	*1 tbsp*	*1 tbsp*
Wholewheat flour	*75 g*	*3 oz*	*¾ cup*
Vegetable margarine	*75 g*	*3 oz*	*⅓ cup*
Brown sugar	*100 g*	*4 oz*	*⅔ cup*
Desiccated (shredded)			
coconut	*50 g*	*2 oz*	*⅔ cup*

1.   To make the pastry, place the flour and baking powder in a bowl and rub (cut) in the margarine until the mixture resembles breadcrumbs. Make a well in the centre, add the water and mix until a dough forms. Cover and chill for at least 30 minutes.

2.   Meanwhile, for the filling, wash the apples, core and cut into slices. Mix with the lemon juice and set aside.

3.   To make the filling, place the flour in a bowl and rub (cut) in the margarine. Stir in the sugar and coconut.

4.   Roll out the pastry on a lightly floured surface and use to line a 20 cm/8 inch flan tin (pie pan).

5.   Fill with the drained apples, sprinkle on the crumb mixture and bake the flan in a preheated oven at 220°C/425°F/Gas Mark 7 for 15 minutes. Lower heat to 170°C/325°F/Gas Mark 3 for a further 25 minutes, or until the apples are tender and the crumble topping lightly browned.

Did you know?
Apples contain starch but it turns to sugar as they ripen.

tutti frutti trifle

Serves 4

Ingredients	Metric	Imperial	American
Weetabix	*6*	*6*	*6*
Eating apples, cored and sliced	*2*	*2*	*2*
Oranges, peeled and segmented	*2*	*2*	*2*
Small grapefruit, peeled and segmented	*1*	*1*	*1*
Banana, peeled and sliced	*1*	*1*	*1*
Pear, cored and chopped	*1*	*1*	*1*
Seedless grapes	*50 g*	*2 oz*	*½ cup*
Fruit juice	*300 ml*	*½ pint*	*1¼ cups*
Agar-agar	*1 tsp*	*1 tsp*	*1 tsp*
Free-range eggs	*2*	*2*	*2*
Brown sugar	*1 tbsp*	*1 tbsp*	*1 tbsp*
Skimmed milk or soya milk	*300 ml*	*½ pint*	*1¼ cups*
Vanilla extract	*1 tsp*	*1 tsp*	*1 tsp*

1.   Crumble the Weetabix and place in the bottom of a glass serving bowl. Arrange the apple slices over the Weetabix. Add all the remaining fruit except the grapes.

2.   Heat the fruit juice and stir in the agar-agar. Leave to cool slightly, then pour over the fruit. Leave to set.

3.   Whisk the eggs and sugar together in a small saucepan. Stir in the milk and vanilla and heat very gently until a thick custard forms. Pour over the trifle and leave to cool.

4.　When the custard is cold, decorate with the grapes.

Variation
For a very special occasion a little whipped low-fat cream could be added to the trifle.

Did you know?
Gelatine is a substance which comes from the bones of animals. Agar-agar is the vegetarian alternative derived from sea vegetables.

baked pineapple parcels

Serves 4

Ingredients	Metric	Imperial	American
Dried apricots	100 g	4 oz	⅔ cup
Apple juice	300 ml	½ pint	1¼ cups
Vegetable margarine	25 g	1 oz	2 tbsp
Vanilla extract	1 tsp	1 tsp	1 tsp
Fresh or canned (in natural juice) pineapple slices	6	6	6
Mint leaves to decorate			

1.   Soak the apricots in the apple juice for several hours or overnight.

2.   When hydrated, place the apricots in a blender or food processor with the margarine and vanilla extract. Blend until smooth.

3.   Cut the pineapple into cubes and divide into four portions. Cut four pieces of foil about 20 cm/ 8 inches square and place a portion of fruit in the centre of each. Spoon 2 tbsp apricot sauce over the pineapple and close the parcels.

4.   Place on a baking tray and bake in a preheated oven at 180°C/350°F/Gas Mark 4 for 20 minutes.

5.   Serve in the parcels, decorated with a few mint leaves.

Did you know?
The first pineapple in England was reputed to have been grown at Dorney in Buckinghamshire. The village pub is still called 'The Pineapple'.

millet and apricot pudding

Serves 4

Ingredients	Metric	Imperial	American
Dried apricots,			
roughly chopped	*75 g*	*3 oz*	*½ cup*
Apple juice concentrate	*3 tbsp*	*3 tbsp*	*3 tbsp*
Skimmed milk or			
soya milk	*600 ml*	*1 pint*	*2½ cups*
Millet	*100 g*	*4 oz*	*¼ lb*
Desiccated (shredded)			
coconut	*25 g*	*1 oz*	*⅓ cup*
Vanilla extract	*1 tsp*	*1 tsp*	*1 tsp*
Honey	*40 g*	*1½ oz*	*2¼ tbsp*

1. Leave the apricots to soak in the apple juice concentrate for 2–3 hours.
2. Put the milk and millet into a saucepan and bring to the boil. Lower the heat and simmer gently for 10 minutes. Remove from the heat and stir in the coconut, vanilla, honey and apricots.
3. Pour the pudding into an ovenproof dish and bake in a preheated oven at 180°C/350°F/Gas Mark 4 for about 1 hour, or until lightly browned.

Variation
Experiment with different dried fruits depending on the young persons' tastes. Figs or peaches make exciting alternatives.

Did you know?
Millet is of higher nutritional value than most other grains. Serve it as a change from rice pudding.

citrus pancakes

Makes 4

Ingredients	Metric	Imperial	American
Wholewheat flour	*100 g*	*4 oz*	*1 cup*
Free-range eggs	*2*	*2*	*2*
Skimmed milk or			
soya milk	*300 ml*	*½ pint*	*1¼ cups*
Grated rind of 1 orange			
Satsumas, peeled and			
segmented	*4*	*4*	*4*
Clear honey	*1 tbsp*	*1 tbsp*	*1 tbsp*
Sunflower oil for frying			
Ground hazelnuts	*50 g*	*2 oz*	*½ cup*

1.   Sift the flour into a bowl. Make a well in the centre and beat in the eggs one at a time. Gradually beat in the milk and orange rind. Leave the batter aside for 1 hour.
2.   Mix the satsumas with the honey. Heat a little oil in a small frying pan (skillet) and pour in a little of the batter, making sure the pan is evenly coated. Cook until set, then flip the pancake (crêpe) over and cook the second side.
3.   Spoon a portion of satsuma and honey onto the pancake and fold over. Heat through for 2–3 minutes, then transfer to a heated plate and keep warm while cooking the remaining pancakes.
4.   Sprinkle each pancake with ground hazelnuts and serve with Greek-style yoghurt.

Did you know?
Brittany claims to make the finest pancakes or crêpes and they use buckwheat flour.

sarah's fruit pudding

Serves 8

Ingredients	Metric	Imperial	American
Self-raising wholewheat flour	350 g	12 oz	3 cups
Mixed spice	1 tsp	1 tsp	1 tsp
Vegetable margarine	225 g	8 oz	1 cup
Brown sugar	100 g	4 oz	⅔ cup
Free-range eggs	3	3	3
Skimmed milk or soya milk	4 tbsp	4 tbsp	4 tbsp
Sultanas (golden raisins)	100 g	4 oz	⅔ cup
Eating apples, cored and diced	450 g	1 lb	1 lb

1. Place the flour and spice in a bowl and rub (cut) in the margarine until the mixture resembles breadcrumbs. Stir in the sugar, the eggs, one at a time, and finally the milk. Add the sultanas, mixing lightly.
2. Place one third of the mixture in the bottom of a greased 23 cm/9 inch cake tin (pan). Add a layer of half the diced apple. Continue the layers, ending with a layer of cake mixture.
3. Bake in a preheated oven at 180°C/350°F/Gas Mark 4 for 1¼ hours or until firm to the touch.
4. Serve warm with Greek-style yoghurt.

Did you know?
The bright shiny skins of apples are often the result of waxing designed to lure the shopper. Always wash the skins thoroughly before eating.

brown bread ice cream

Serves 4

Ingredients	Metric	Imperial	American
Brown sugar	*100 g*	*4 oz*	*⅔ cup*
Wholewheat breadcrumbs	*50 g*	*2 oz*	*1 cup*
Low-fat double (heavy)			
cream	*300 ml*	*8 oz*	*1¼ cups*
Frozen soft fruits	*225 g*	*8 oz*	*½ lb*
Plain yoghurt	*300 ml*	*½ pint*	*1¼ cups*

1.   Mix half the sugar with the breadcrumbs, spread in a shallow ovenproof dish and toast in a preheated oven at 220°C/425°F/Gas Mark 7 until browned and crisp.

2.   Gently heat the cream and remaining sugar in a saucepan. Do not boil. Stir in the fruit and then the yoghurt. When the mixture is well blended, add the breadcrumbs and stir well.

3.   Pour into a 600 ml/1 pint/2½ cup freezer container and freeze.

4.   Serve in individual dishes with extra fresh fruit.

Did you know?
Yoghurt is a living food containing live bacteria. These bacteria are thought to have a beneficial effect on the digestive system by encouraging the growth of bacteria which prevent disease-forming organisms.

summer fruit charlotte

Serves 4

Ingredients	Metric	Imperial	American
Wholewheat bread slices	*8*	*8*	*8*
Apple jelly	*2 tbsp*	*2 tbsp*	*2 tbsp*
Mixed summer fruits (e.g. raspberries, straw- berries, redcurrants, etc.)	*450 g*	*1 lb*	*1 lb*
Plain yoghurt	*225 ml*	*8 fl oz*	*1 cup*
Brown sugar	*75 g*	*3 oz*	*½ cup*

1.   Spread the bread with the apple jelly and cut each slice in four. Arrange 10 pieces of bread in the bottom of an ovenproof dish.
2.   Mix the fruit, yoghurt and sugar and spread half of the mixture over the bread. Place another layer of bread on top and then the remaining fruit. Finish with a layer of bread, jellied side uppermost.
3.   Bake in a preheated oven at 190°C/375°F/Gas Mark 5 for 25-30 minutes or until crusty and brown.

Note
Any puréed fresh or dried fruit may be substituted for the summer fruits in this charlotte.

Did you know?
Fruit picked in the evening is richer in vitamin C than that harvested earlier in the day. So if you 'pick your own' it's better to go later in the day.

apricot and apple smoothie

Serves 4

Ingredients	Metric	Imperial	American
Apple juice concentrate	*1 tbsp*	*1 tbsp*	*1 tbsp*
Water	*600 ml*	*1 pint*	*2½ cups*
Brown sugar	*50 g*	*2 oz*	*⅓ cup*
Dried apricots	*225 g*	*8 oz*	*1⅓ cups*
Eating apples, cored and roughly chopped	*2*	*2*	*2*
Arrowroot	*1 tbsp*	*1 tbsp*	*1 tbsp*
Sesame (benne) seeds	*25 g*	*1 oz*	*¼ cup*

1.   Mix the apple juice concentrate with the water and sugar and pour over the apricots in a bowl. Leave to soak overnight.

2.   Pour the dried apricot mixture into a saucepan, bring to the boil and cook for about 15 minutes, or until tender. Add the apples and continue cooking until the apples are soft. Allow to cool and then purée in a blender or food processor.

3.   In a small bowl, mix the arrowroot with a little water to form a smooth paste. Add to the fruit, stirring continuously, and bring to the boil. When the purée thickens, remove from the heat and leave to cool slightly before pouring into individual dishes. Sprinkle the sesame seeds over the top and serve with shortbread biscuits.

Did you know?
The Hunza tribe, famous for its longevity, eats a diet consisting of large quantities of apricots.

fruit and nut salad

This fruit salad is delicious served with plain or Greek-style yoghurt. If you are still trying to wean the children off sugar, stir a little honey into the yoghurt.

Serves 2

Ingredients	Metric	Imperial	American
Apple juice concentrate	*2 tbsp*	*2 tbsp*	*2 tbsp*
Water	*300 ml*	*½ pint*	*1¼ cups*
Lemon juice	*1 tsp*	*1 tsp*	*1 tsp*
Orange, peeled and cut in wedges	*1*	*1*	*1*
Red eating apple, cored and sliced	*1*	*1*	*1*
Green eating apple, cored and sliced	*1*	*1*	*1*
Banana, peeled and sliced	*1*	*1*	*1*
Pineapple slice, cut in wedges	*1*	*1*	*1*
Black or green grapes, seeded	*100 g*	*4 oz*	*1 cup*
Chopped walnuts	*50 g*	*2 oz*	*½ cup*

1.   Dilute the apple juice concentrate with the water and stir in the lemon juice.

2.   Place all the prepared fruit in a serving bowl and pour over the juice. Chill the salad, and, just before serving, stir in the walnuts.

Did you know?
Fruit supplies us with many essential minerals not found in other foods.

raisin slices

Makes 16

Ingredients	Metric	Imperial	American
Raisins	225 g	8 oz	1⅓ cups
Boiling water	600 ml	1 pint	2½ cups
Marmalade	3 tbsp	3 tbsp	3 tbsp
Self-raising wholewheat flour	225 g	8 oz	2 cups
Vegetable margarine	75 g	3 oz	⅓ cup
Brown sugar	25 g	1 oz	2 tbsp
Free-range egg	1	1	1
Skimmed milk or soya milk	3–4 tbsp	3–4 tbsp	3–4 tbsp
Extra milk for brushing			
Poppy seeds	1 tbsp	1 tbsp	1 tbsp

1. Cover the raisins with the boiling water and leave to stand for 10 minutes. Drain and stir in the marmalade.

2. Place the flour in a bowl and rub (cut) in the margarine until the mixture resembles bread-crumbs. Stir in the sugar.

3. Beat the egg and milk together and pour onto the crumb mixture. Stir lightly to form a soft dough. Cut the dough in half. On a lightly floured surface, roll out one half of dough and use to line a greased 27 × 18 cm/11 × 7 inch baking tin (pan). Spread the raisin mixture over this.

4. Roll out the remaining dough and use to cover the raisins. Brush with milk and sprinkle with poppy seeds.

5. Bake in a preheated oven at 220°C/425°F/Gas Mark 7 for 25 minutes or until golden brown. Serve the slices warm with Greek-style yoghurt.

Did you know?
Raisins are high in natural sugars and will provide just as much energy as commercial sweet products.

peach surprise

Serves 4

Ingredients	Metric	Imperial	American
Ricotta cheese	100 g	4 oz	½ cup
Chopped mixed nuts	50 g	2 oz	½ cup
Lemon juice	squeeze	squeeze	squeeze
Grated orange rind	1 tsp	1 tsp	1 tsp
Honey	1 tbsp	1 tbsp	1 tbsp
Large, ripe peaches, halved and stoned (pitted)	4	4	4
Black grapes	4	4	4

1. Mix together the cheese and nuts in a bowl. Stir in the lemon juice, orange rind and honey.
2. Place each peach on a plate, hollow sides up. Fill with the cheese mixture and top with a grape.

Did you know?
Ricotta is a low-fat cheese made with skimmed milk. In general, soft cheeses have a lower fat content than hard cheeses, such as Cheddar.

raspberry roll

Serves 10

Ingredients	Metric	Imperial	American
Free-range eggs	3	3	3
Brown sugar	75 g	3 oz	½ cup
Ground hazelnuts	75 g	3 oz	¾ cup
Self-raising wholewheat flour	100 g	4 oz	1 cup
Hot water	1 tbsp	1 tbsp	1 tbsp
Sesame (benne) seeds	1 tbsp	1 tbsp	1 tbsp
Raspberries	225 g	8 oz	½ lb
Plain Greek-style yoghurt	450 g	1 lb	1 lb

1. Whisk the eggs and sugar together in a bowl until thick and creamy.
2. Mix together the nuts and flour and fold half into the eggs. Add the remaining nuts and flour, then stir in the water.
3. Pour the mixture into a greased and lined Swiss roll tin (jelly roll pan) measuring 23 × 30 cm/9 × 12 inches. Bake in a preheated oven at 200°C/400°F/Gas Mark 6 for 10 minutes, or until well risen and brown. Turn the cake out onto greaseproof (waxed) paper sprinkled with sesame seeds and leave to cool.
4. Chop the raspberries and stir them into the Greek-style yoghurt. Spread onto the Swiss roll and roll up firmly. Cover with cling film (plastic wrap) and chill before serving.

Did you know?
Raspberries contain the same amount of vitamin C as raw radishes.

strawberry and tofu fool

Serves 3-4

Ingredients	Metric	Imperial	American
Fresh strawberries, hulled	*225 g*	*8 oz*	*½ lb*
Silken tofu	*225 g*	*8 oz*	*½ lb*
Clear honey	*2 tbsp*	*2 tbsp*	*2 tbsp*
Lemon juice	*2 tsp*	*2 tsp*	*2 tsp*

1.   Reserve 3–4 strawberries for decoration and place the remainder in a blender or food processor. Blend very briefly, then pour into a bowl.
2.   Place the tofu, honey and lemon juice in the blender or food processor and blend until smooth. Pour onto the strawberries and stir to mix.
3.   Pour the purée into dessert glasses and chill. Just before serving, place a whole strawberry on top of each.

Variation
This fool is equally delicious with soft fruits, such as blackcurrants, raspberries, redcurrants, etc.

Did you know?
There's more vitamin C in strawberries than oranges.

carob pears

Serves 4

Ingredients	Metric	Imperial	American
Ripe pears	*4*	*4*	*4*
Raisins	*25 g*	*1 oz*	*3 tbsp*
Chopped walnuts	*25 g*	*1 oz*	*¼ cup*
Plain carob bar	*40 g*	*1½ oz*	*1½ oz*
Free-range egg, separated	*1*	*1*	*1*
Fresh mint leaves, to decorate	*4*	*4*	*4*

1.   Peel and core the pears, leaving the stalks intact. Poach the pears lightly in water, until just tender. Leave to cool.

2.   Mix the raisins and nuts together and use to fill the pear cavities.

3.   Melt the carob in 2 tbsp of water, stirring continuously. Allow to cool slightly, then blend in the egg yolk.

4.   Whisk the egg white until stiff and fold into the carob mixture.

5.   Place the pears on a pretty serving dish and dribble the carob sauce over them. Decorate the top of each with a mint leaf.

Did you know?
The seeds of the carob bean were used by early traders to weigh gold. This is thought to be the origin of our measurement for gold – the 'carat'.

CHAPTER 9

the cookie JAR

m any families have to endure the lure of the cookie jar. It sits innocently on the bench of most kitchens and it is a main priority to keep it filled to the brim.

For years I used to feel guilty because I refused to buy biscuits, and I remember children who visited staring in wide-eyed disbelief when they were offered bread instead. How many youngsters have been labelled 'faddy eaters' when they were really just too full of cookies to make room for a proper meal?

Times, I hope, have changed and now it is much more likely to be the owner of the cookie jar who feels the guilt. If you still do, this chapter of recipes offers you a way out, an opportunity to escape from the clutches of the white sugar pedlars. Gradually replace your cookies with these more nutritious alternatives until your youngsters lose their craving for their next sugar 'fix'.

banana and sunflower cookies

Makes 20

Ingredients	Metric	Imperial	American
Vegetable margarine	*50 g*	*2 oz*	*¼ cup*
Brown sugar	*50 g*	*2 oz*	*⅓ cup*
Rolled oats	*100 g*	*4 oz*	*1 cup*
Sunflower seeds	*50 g*	*2 oz*	*½ cup*
Sultanas (golden raisins)	*50 g*	*2 oz*	*⅓ cup*
Banana, peeled and mashed	*1*	*1*	*1*
Free-range egg, beaten	*1*	*1*	*1*

1.   Melt the margarine and sugar together in a saucepan and stir in the oats, seeds, sultanas and mashed banana. Bind the mixture with the beaten egg.

2.   Drop large teaspoonfuls of the mixture at intervals on greased baking sheets. Bake in a preheated oven at 180°C/350°F/Gas Mark 4 for 10–15 minutes. Leave to cool on the baking sheets.

3.   When cold, remove the cookies from the baking sheets and store in an airtight container.

Did you know?
Sunflower seeds are a good source of unsaturated fats. There are over 60 varieties of sunflower.

coconut and sesame biscuits

Makes 16

Ingredients	Metric	Imperial	American
Desiccated (shredded) coconut	100 g	4 oz	1⅓ cups
Soya flour	25 g	1 oz	¼ cup
Brown sugar	100 g	4 oz	⅔ cup
Rolled oats	100 g	4 oz	1 cup
Sesame (benne) seeds	25 g	1 oz	¼ cup
Vegetable margarine	100 g	4 oz	½ cup
Vanilla extract	1 tsp	1 tsp	1 tsp

1.   Mix the coconut, flour, sugar, oats and sesame seeds together in a large bowl.

2.   Melt the margarine in a saucepan and pour over the dry ingredients. Stir in the vanilla extract.

3.   Press the mixture into a greased 27 × 18 cm/ 11 × 7 inch baking tray. Bake in a preheated oven at 190°C/375°F/Gas Mark 5 for 20–30 minutes, or until browned.

4.   Mark the biscuit into fingers and leave to cool in the baking tray. Store in an airtight container.

Did you know?
Queen Nefertiti considered sesame oil to be the finest cosmetic.

sesame biscuits

Makes 20–30

Ingredients	Metric	Imperial	American
Plain (all-purpose) wholewheat flour	225 g	8 oz	2 cups
Baking powder	1 tsp	1 tsp	1 tsp
Ground cinnamon	1 tsp	1 tsp	1 tsp
Grated rind of 1 lemon			
Vegetable margarine	175 g	6 oz	¾ cup
Sesame (benne) seeds	25 g	1 oz	¼ cup
Brown sugar	25 g	1 oz	2 tbsp
Free-range egg	1	1	1
Skimmed milk or soya milk	5 tbsp	5 tbsp	5 tbsp

1. Sift together the flour, baking powder and cinnamon into a bowl and stir in the lemon rind. Rub (cut) in the margarine until the mixture resembles breadcrumbs. Stir in the sesame seeds and sugar.

2. Beat the egg and mix with the milk. Pour onto the crumb mixture and mix to a dough. Chill for 1 hour.

3. Roll out the dough and cut out biscuits with a fancy 5 cm/2 inch pastry cutter. Lay the biscuits on greased baking sheets and bake in a preheated oven at 180°C/350°F/Gas Mark 4 for 20 minutes. Leave to cool on the baking sheets, then, when cold, store in an airtight container.

Did you know?
Sesame seeds are known as 'brain food'. They contain 10 times as much calcium as milk.

almond munchies

Makes 20

Ingredients	Metric	Imperial	American
Plain (all-purpose) wholewheat flour	50 g	2 oz	½ cup
Wholewheat semolina (farina)	100 g	4 oz	⅔ cup
Vegetable margarine	100 g	4 oz	½ cup
Ground almonds	50 g	2 oz	½ cup
Brown sugar	75 g	3 oz	½ cup
Skimmed milk or soya milk	3 tbsp	3 tbsp	3 tbsp
Whole blanched almonds, split in half	10	10	10

1.   Place the flour and semolina in a bowl and rub (cut) in the margarine until the mixture resembles breadcrumbs. Stir in the ground almonds and sugar, pour on the milk and mix to a smooth dough.

2.   Roll out the dough to 5 mm/¼ inch thick and cut into biscuits using a 5 cm/2 inch pastry cutter. Place on greased baking sheets and press an almond half onto each biscuit. Bake in a preheated oven at 190°C/375°F/Gas Mark 5 for 15 minutes, or until lightly browned.

3.   Leave to cool on the baking sheets.

Did you know?
Semolina is a product of the starchy part of the wheat grain.

carob pinwheels

Makes 20

Ingredients	Metric	Imperial	American
Vegetable margarine	*100 g*	*4 oz*	*½ cup*
Brown sugar	*75 g*	*3 oz*	*½ cup*
Free-range egg, beaten	*1*	*1*	*1*
Plain (all-purpose)			
wholewheat flour	*175 g*	*6 oz*	*1½ cups*
Grated lemon rind	*1 tsp*	*1 tsp*	*1 tsp*
Carob powder	*50 g*	*2 oz*	*½ cup*
Milk for brushing			

1.   Place the margarine and sugar in a bowl and cream together until light and fluffy. Beat in the egg, a little at a time, beating well after each addition. If the mixture curdles, add 1 tbsp flour.

2.   Divide the mixture between two bowls. Sift half the flour into one bowl, add the lemon rind and stir until incorporated. Sift the remaining flour and carob powder together into the second bowl and mix well.

3.   On a lightly floured surface, roll out the pale-coloured dough to form an oblong 5 mm/¼ inch thick. Roll out the carob dough to the same size.

4.   Lightly brush the surface of the first piece of dough with milk and lay the other piece on top. Roll up like a Swiss (jelly) roll, cover and chill for 30 minutes.

5. With a sharp knife, slice the roll into biscuits 5 mm/¼ inch thick. Place on greased baking sheets and bake in a preheated oven at 180°C/350°F/Gas Mark 4 for about 20 minutes. Remove from the baking sheets when cool and store in an airtight container.

Did you know?
The best flour is 'stoneground' because it is ground all in one process without any of the bran or wheatgerm being removed.

honey and muesli shortbread

Makes 16

Ingredients	Metric	Imperial	American
Honey	*225 g*	*8 oz*	*⅔ cup*
Vegetable margarine	*175 g*	*6 oz*	*⅔ cup*
Muesli (sugar-free)	*100 g*	*4 oz*	*¼ lb*
Plain (all-purpose)			
* wholewheat flour*	*225 g*	*8 oz*	*2 cups*

1. In a saucepan, heat the honey and margarine together over a low heat until the margarine has melted. Stir in the muesli and flour.
2. Press the mixture into a greased 27 × 18 cm/ 11 × 7 inch baking tray. Smooth the surface and bake in a preheated oven at 180°C/350°F/Gas Mark 4 for 25 minutes.
3. Remove from the oven and carefully mark out the biscuits with a knife. Leave them in the baking tray until quite cold.

Did you know?
Darker honeys contain more minerals than lighter honeys.

no-sugar fruit and nut bar

Makes 16

Ingredients	Metric	Imperial	American
Dried dates, soaked overnight and drained	175 g	6 oz	1 cup
Dried apricots, soaked overnight and drained	175 g	6 oz	1 cup
Water	300 ml	½ pint	1¼ cups
Apple juice concentrate	6 tbsp	6 tbsp	6 tbsp
Plain (all-purpose) wholewheat flour	150 g	5 oz	1¼ cups
Baking powder	1 tsp	1 tsp	1 tsp
Rolled oats	175 g	6 oz	1½ cups
Vegetable margarine	75 g	3 oz	⅓ cup
Ripe bananas, mashed	3	3	3
Peanuts	100 g	4 oz	½ cup

1. Place the dried fruit, water and apple juice concentrate in a saucepan, bring to the boil and simmer for about 30 minutes, or until tender.

2. Place the flour, baking powder and oats in a bowl and rub (cut) in the margarine until the mixture resembles breadcrumbs. Stir in the mashed banana and mix to form a dough.

3. Press half the dough into the bottom of a greased 27 × 18 cm/11 × 7 inch baking tray. Pour the fruit mixture on top and sprinkle with the peanuts. Top with the remaining dough. Bake in a preheated oven at 220°C/425°F/Gas Mark 7 for 25 minutes.

4. Cut into fingers and leave to cool in the baking tray. Store in an airtight container.

carob chip cookies

Makes 20

Ingredients	Metric	Imperial	American
Vegetable margarine	*75 g*	*3 oz*	*⅓ cup*
Brown sugar	*100 g*	*4 oz*	*⅔ cup*
Free-range egg	*1*	*1*	*1*
Self-raising wholewheat flour	*175 g*	*6 oz*	*1½ cups*
Carob chips	*100 g*	*4 oz*	*¼ lb*

1. Place the margarine and sugar in a bowl and cream together until light and fluffy. Beat in the egg and beat until the mixture returns to its original consistency. Fold in the flour and carob chips.

2. Drop spoonfuls of the mixture onto greased baking sheets. Bake in a preheated oven at 180°C/ 350°F/Gas Mark 4 for 10–15 minutes, or until browned.

3. Allow to cool before removing from baking sheets.

Did you know?
Unlike chocolate, carob does not contain caffeine. Migraine sufferers unable to eat chocolate often enjoy carob.

fruity carob flapjacks

Makes 16

Ingredients	Metric	Imperial	American
Golden (light corn) syrup	120 ml	4 fl oz	½ cup
Corn oil	120 ml	4 fl oz	½ cup
Rolled oats	350 g	12 oz	3 cups
Grated rind and juice of 1 lemon			
Carob powder	1 tbsp	1 tbsp	1 tbsp

1.   Place the syrup and oil in a saucepan and heat gently over a low heat. Add all the remaining ingredients and stir well.

2.   Press the mixture into a greased and lined 27 × 18 cm/11 × 7 inch baking tray. Bake in a preheated oven at 200°C/400°F/Gas Mark 6 for 25 minutes.

3.   Cut the flapjack into fingers and leave to cool in the tray.

Did you know?
Carob is also known as St. John's bread. John the Baptist is said to have lived on it during his sojourn in the desert.

peanut butter cookies

Makes 20

Ingredients	Metric	Imperial	American
Vegetable margarine	*50 g*	*2 oz*	*¼ cup*
Brown sugar	*75 g*	*3 oz*	*½ cup*
Crunchy peanut butter	*75 g*	*3 oz*	*6 tbsp*
Grated orange rind	*1 tsp*	*1 tsp*	*1 tsp*
Free-range egg	*1*	*1*	*1*
Self-raising wholewheat flour	*100 g*	*4 oz*	*1 cup*

1.   Place the margarine and sugar in a bowl and cream together until light and fluffy. Beat in the peanut butter and orange rind. Beat in the egg, then stir in the flour to give a stiff dough.

2.   Drop spoonfuls of the mixture onto greased baking sheets. Bake in a preheated oven at 180°C/ 350°F/Gas Mark 4 for about 25 minutes, or until lightly browned.

3.   Leave to cool on the baking sheets.

Did you know?
Peanuts are a rich source of vitamin B.

peanut and raisin cookies

Makes 12

Ingredients	Metric	Imperial	American
Self-raising wholewheat flour	175 g	6 oz	1½ cups
Vegetable margarine	50 g	2 oz	¼ cup
Apple juice concentrate	2 tbsp	2 tbsp	2 tbsp
Crunchy peanut butter	75 g	3 oz	6 tbsp
Brown sugar	50 g	2 oz	⅓ cup
Raisins	50 g	2 oz	⅓ cup

1. Place the flour in a bowl and rub (cut) in the margarine until the mixture resembles bread-crumbs.

2. Stir the apple juice concentrate into the peanut butter with the sugar. Add to the crumb mixture with the raisins. If the mixture is too dry, add a little milk.

3. Divide the mixture into walnut-sized pieces and place, evenly-spaced, on a greased baking sheet. Flatten each cookie slightly with the back of a fork.

4. Bake in a preheated oven at 180°C/350°F/Gas Mark 4 for 10-15 minutes. Cool on a wire rack and store in an airtight container.

Did you know?
Peanuts contain more protein than other nuts.

CHAPTER 10

cook your **OWN**

|t| his chapter is for the youngsters of the family –
to give you a chance to discover for yourselves the
benefit and enjoyment to be gained from a whole-
food, vegetarian approach to eating. Perhaps you
have heard friends and family talking about cutting
down on fat, sugar and salt and you will surely be
familiar with the word 'fibre'. There can't be many
families without at least one member who has tried
the 'F Plan Diet'. To help you understand it all, it's a
good idea to try a bit of cooking for yourselves, so
that you can really see what changes are being
made.

You can derive a great deal of satisfaction and
pleasure from using natural ingredients to cook
delicious meals. Do remember that cooking is an art
and, although I advise sticking to the recipes to begin
with, the real excitement comes from creating your
own dishes.

Have fun with the recipes and remember to leave
the kitchen as you found it. A tidy cook will almost
certainly be asked to return.

sprout your own

You don't need to own a garden to be able to grow your own food. Seeds, grains, beans and lentils can all be grown cheaply and easily on a kitchen windowsill. All they require is a little tender loving care!

To make 450 g/1 lb of beansprouts, you will need 1 large glass jar (the beans will increase in volume by about 7–8 times); a piece of muslin (cheesecloth) to cover the neck of the jar; a piece of string; 50 g/2 oz/ ¼ cup dried beans.

1.   Wash the beans and pick out any foreign bodies or discoloured beans. Place them in the bottom of the jar and cover with warm water.

2.   Tie the muslin over the top of the jar with the string, and leave to stand in a warm place overnight. (The airing cupboard is ideal.)

3.   Next morning, strain off the water, rinse with more water and leave the beans just damp. Stand the jar on a windowsill in a warm room where you won't forget it.

4.   Repeat the rinsing process every morning and evening until you have sprouts at least 5 cm/ 2 inches long. The length of time taken to germinate will depend upon the age of the beans and the temperature of the room. As a rough guide, beans will take 5–7 days, grains 7–9 days and seeds 2–3 days.

5.   Store the sprouts in a plastic bag in the refrigerator and use as required in salads, sandwiches, etc.

The following are the most commonly sprouted:

Pulses – soya beans, chick-peas, mung beans, adzuki beans and lentils.

Grains – wheat, barley and oats.

Seeds – pumpkin, sesame, sunflower, alfalfa, fenugreek and mustard.

pumpkin and apple coleslaw

Serves 4

Ingredients	Metric	Imperial	American
Shredded white cabbage, small	1	1	1
Chopped onion, small	1	1	1
Grated carrot, medium-size	1	1	1
Celery stalks, sliced	2	2	2
Red eating apple, cored and chopped	1	1	1
Chopped fresh parsley	1 tbsp	1 tbsp	1 tbsp
Pumpkin seeds	25 g	1 oz	¼ cup
Dressing			
Low-fat mayonnaise	50 ml	2 fl oz	¼ cup
Lemon juice	1 tbsp	1 tbsp	1 tbsp
Plain yoghurt	50 ml	2 fl oz	¼ cup

1. To make the dressing, beat together the mayonnaise, lemon juice and yoghurt.

2. In a large bowl, mix together the cabbage, onion, carrot, celery, apple and parsley. Pour over the mayonnaise dressing and stir well to coat evenly.

3. Sprinkle the pumpkin seeds over the top and serve with your favourite cheese or nuts.

Did you know?
Vegetables eaten raw not only exercise your jaws, but they also contain all the nutrients which would otherwise leach out into cooking water.

bubble and beans

Makes 4

Ingredients	Metric	Imperial	American
Potatoes, scrubbed	*700 g*	*1½ lb*	*1½ lb*
Vegetable margarine	*25 g*	*1 oz*	*2 tbsp*
Tahini	*1 tbsp*	*1 tbsp*	*1 tbsp*
Soya flour	*50 g*	*2 oz*	*½ cup*
Chopped onion	*1*	*1*	*1*
Cooked cabbage	*225 g*	*8 oz*	*1⅓ cups*
Pinto beans, cooked	*100 g*	*4 oz*	*¼ lb*
Cheddar cheese, grated	*50 g*	*2 oz*	*½ cup*
Fresh parsley sprigs to garnish			

1. Place four small ramekin dishes (custard cups) on a baking sheet.
2. Cut the potatoes in quarters and cook in boiling water for 15–20 minutes, or until tender. Remove the skins and mash with the margarine. (If you can borrow a blender or food processor you can successfully mash the potatoes in their skins.)
3. Stir in the tahini, soya flour, onion and cabbage and mix well.
4. Put a spoonful of the beans in the base of each ramekin and spoon the potato on top. Sprinkle with the grated cheese and bake in a preheated oven at 200°C/400°F/Gas Mark 6 for 15–20 minutes, or until bubbling.
5. Serve hot, garnished with a sprig of fresh parsley.

Did you know?
Tahini has been a favourite spread of the people of the Near East and Greece for centuries. We in the west have only recently discovered it.

broody potatoes

Serves 4

Ingredients	Metric	Imperial	American
Medium-size old potatoes	*4*	*4*	*4*
Vegetable margarine	*25 g*	*1 oz*	*2 tbsp*
Skimmed milk or			
soya milk	*2 tbsp*	*2 tbsp*	*2 tbsp*
Chopped fresh chives	*1 tbsp*	*1 tbsp*	*1 tbsp*
Grated onion, small	*1*	*1*	*1*
Tahini	*1 tbsp*	*1 tbsp*	*1 tbsp*
Free-range eggs	*4*	*4*	*4*
Sesame (benne) seeds	*1 tbsp*	*1 tbsp*	*1 tbsp*

1.   Scrub the potatoes and, using a sharp knife, mark a ring around the top. Bake in a preheated oven at 220°C/425°F/Gas Mark 7 for 45 minutes–1 hour, or until soft. Remove from the oven and reduce the oven temperature to 180°C/350°F/Gas Mark 4.

2.   Allow the potatoes to cool slightly, then cut off the tops. Scoop out the cooked potato into a bowl and mash with the margarine and milk. Add the chives and onion and blend in the tahini.

3.   Half fill each empty potato skin with the filling and press down well. Carefully break an egg into each potato, place on a greased baking sheet and return to the oven. Bake for 15 minutes, or until the egg is set.

4. Place the leftover potato mixture in a piping (pastry) bag fitted with a star nozzle and use to decorate the top of each potato with rosettes. Sprinkle with sesame seeds and brown under the grill. Serve with grilled tomatoes.

Did you know?
Sir Francis Drake saw the Indians in Chile eating potatoes in 1577, but it was not until about 1588 that Sir Walter Raleigh is supposed to have introduced them to Ireland and Britain.

baked bean dip

Serves 4

Ingredients	Metric	Imperial	American
Canned baked beans	*450 g*	*1 lb*	*1 lb*
Tomato ketchup	*100 g*	*4 oz*	*8 tbsp*
Chopped onion, small	*1*	*1*	*1*
Plain yoghurt	*120 ml*	*4 fl oz*	*½ cup*
Chopped cucumber	*2 tbsp*	*2 tbsp*	*2 tbsp*

1. Blend all the ingredients together in a small bowl. If you prefer a smoother dip, ask permission to use a blender or food processor and blend for 2 minutes.
2. Spoon the dip into four individual dishes and garnish with chopped cucumber.
3. Serve with raw vegetables and low-fat crisps (chips) for dipping.

Did you know?
Mashed and fried beans are a major part of Mexican cooking, where they are called re-fried beans.

'alternative' chips

Eating healthily doesn't mean you can never so much as look at chips (French fries) again. It's quite permissible to indulge occasionally, and here's a method of creating chips which are low in fat and high in fibre. Remember that all the goodness in potatoes lies just below the skin and if you peel large chunks off you throw most of the nutrients away so it's best not to peel them at all.

Serves 2

Ingredients	Metric	Imperial	American
Large potatoes	*3*	*3*	*3*
Vegetable oil	*1 tbsp*	*1 tbsp*	*1 tbsp*

1. Scrub the potatoes but do not peel them. Cut them into chips.
2. Mix the oil with 1 tbsp water and pour over the chips. Arrange on a baking sheet and bake in a preheated oven at 220°C/425°F/Gas Mark 7 for 30 minutes, or until golden brown.
3. Serve in small bowls with salad.

Did you know?
Potatoes are not fattening but are packed full of carbohydrate which provides us with bags of energy.

onion bundles

Serves 4

Ingredients	Metric	Imperial	American
Plain (all-purpose) wholewheat flour	*100 g*	*4 oz*	*1 cup*
Vegetable margarine	*50 g*	*2 oz*	*¼ cup*
Grated onion	*2 tsp*	*2 tsp*	*2 tsp*
Yeast extract	*1 tsp*	*1 tsp*	*1 tsp*
Hot water	*2 tsp*	*2 tsp*	*2 tsp*
Cold water to mix, if needed			

1. Place the flour in a bowl and rub (cut) in the margarine until the mixture resembles bread-crumbs. Stir in the grated onion.
2. Mix the yeast extract with the hot water and, when diluted, pour onto the crumb mixture. Using a fork, mix lightly until a stiff dough forms. Add extra water if needed.
3. Roll out the pastry on a lightly floured surface to two 20 × 5 cm/8 × 2 inch oblongs. Cut sticks 5 mm/¼ inch thick from one oblong and lay them on a lightly greased baking sheet. Cut circles from the remaining pastry using a 5 cm/2 inch cutter. Using a 4 cm/1½ inch cutter, cut out the centres. lay the pastry rings on the baking sheet.
4. Bake the pastries in a preheated oven at 200°C/400°F/Gas Mark 6 for 10–15 minutes, or until crisp and golden. When cold, place bundles of 4–5 sticks in each ring.

Did you know?
Yeast extract is full of B vitamins.

mexican scone pizzas

Makes 2

Ingredients	Metric	Imperial	American
Base			
Self-raising wholewheat flour	*225 g*	*8 oz*	*2 cups*
Vegetable margarine	*50 g*	*2 oz*	*¼ cup*
Grated cheese	*50 g*	*2 oz*	*½ cup*
Skimmed milk or soya milk	*150 ml*	*¼ pint*	*⅔ cup*
Topping			
Sunflower oil	*1 tbsp*	*1 tbsp*	*1 tbsp*
Chopped onion	*1*	*1*	*1*
Cooked red kidney beans	*100 g*	*4 oz*	*⅔ cup*
Canned tomatoes	*400 g*	*14 oz*	*3½ cups*
Tomato purée (paste)	*2 tbsp*	*2 tbsp*	*2 tbsp*
Oregano	*½ tsp*	*½ tsp*	*½ tsp*
Basil	*½ tsp*	*½ tsp*	*½ tsp*
Mozzarella cheese, sliced	*75 g*	*3 oz*	*¾ cup*

1.   Sift the flour into a bowl and rub in the margarine until the mixture resembles breadcrumbs. Stir in the cheese and use the milk to mix to a stiff dough. On a floured board, cut the dough in half and roll out 2 rounds about 15–20 cm/6–8 inches across. Place on a large greased baking tray.

2.   Heat the oil in a small frying pan (skillet) and sauté the onion until just soft. Mix the beans, tomatoes, purée, oregano and basil in a small bowl. Pour the onions and oil over and mix well.

3. Spread each pizza with sauce. Arrange the Mozzarella on top.
4. Bake in a preheated oven at 200°C/400°F/Gas Mark 6 for 15–30 minutes until brown and bubbling. Serve with mixed salad.

Variations
Experiment with different toppings such as sliced mushrooms, red and green peppers, courgettes and other bean varities.

Did you know?
If you grow basil on your kitchen windowsill you won't be troubled with flies!

'ants on logs'

Serves 4

Ingredients	Metric	Imperial	American
Celery stalks	4	4	4
Crunchy peanut butter	100 g	4 oz	8 tbsp
Raisins	50 g	2 oz	⅓ cup
Celery leaves, to garnish			

1. Cut the celery stalks into 5 cm/2 inch pieces and fill each piece with peanut butter. Decorate with raisins.
2. Serve on a plate garnished with celery leaves.

Did you know?
The darker the vegetable leaf, the more nutrients it contains.

pizza pittas

Makes 2

Ingredients	Metric	Imperial	American
Small round wholewheat pitta breads	2	2	2
Chopped onion, small	1	1	1
Tomato purée (paste)	3 tbsp	3 tbsp	3 tbsp
Small eating apple, cored and chopped	1	1	1
Dried oregano	½ tsp	½ tsp	½ tsp
Water	2 tbsp	2 tbsp	2 tbsp
Cheddar cheese, grated	50 g	2 oz	½ cup
Tomato slices	2	2	2
Chopped fresh parsley to garnish			

1. Place the pitta bread on a greased baking sheet.
2. In a small bowl, mix together the onion, tomato purée, apple and oregano. Thin slightly with the water to make a thick sauce.
3. Spoon half the sauce over each pitta bread, spreading it evenly. Top with grated cheese and slices of tomato.
4. Bake in a preheated oven at 180°C/350°F/Gas Mark 4 for 15 minutes, or until the cheese is bubbling. Remove from the baking sheet and serve sprinkled with parsley.

Did you know?
The first tomatoes originated in Spain and were yellow. Thomas Jefferson is reputed to have grown the first American tomato in 1781.

green and white salad

Serves 4

Ingredients	Metric	Imperial	American
Frozen peas	*225 g*	*8 oz*	*½ lb*
Sesame (benne) oil	*2 tbsp*	*2 tbsp*	*2 tbsp*
Vinegar	*1 tbsp*	*1 tbsp*	*1 tbsp*
Chopped fresh mint or dried mint	*1 tsp*	*1 tsp*	*1 tsp*
Lettuce	*1*	*1*	*1*
Edam cheese, cubed	*100 g*	*4 oz*	*⅔ cup*
Cooked potato, cubed	*100 g*	*4 oz*	*⅔ cup*
Celery stalk, sliced	*1*	*1*	*1*
Chopped onion	*1*	*1*	*1*
Lemon slices, to garnish			

1. Cook the peas in a little boiling water according to package instructions, drain and set aside.

2. Beat the oil and vinegar together and stir in the mint.

3. Line a salad bowl with lettuce leaves and fill with the cheese, potato, celery, onion and peas. Pour over the mint dressing and toss well.

4. Garnish with lemon slices and serve chilled, with wholewheat bread.

Did you know?
Frozen vegetables often show a higher vitamin C content than fresh vegetables. This is because only the best and freshest are frozen.

peanut dip

Serves 4

Ingredients	Metric	Imperial	American
Sesame oil	1 tbsp	1 tbsp	1 tbsp
Small onion, finely chopped	1	1	1
Coconut milk	300 ml	½ pint	1¼ cups
Apple juice	4 tbsp	4 tbsp	4 tbsp
Malt extract	1 tsp	1 tsp	1 tsp
Shoyu	1 tsp	1 tsp	1 tsp
Unsalted peanut butter	175 g	6 oz	¾ cup
Hard-boiled free-range eggs, sliced	2	2	2
Portions of mixed raw vegetables	4	4	4

1.   Heat the oil in a small frying pan and sauté the onion until transparent. Stir in the coconut milk and bring to the boil. Remove from the heat and stir in the apple juice, malt extract and shoyu.

2.   Pour the mixture onto the peanut butter, a little at a time, blending well after each addition.

3.   Arrange egg slices on individual plates with the vegetables. Spoon over some of the peanut sauce.

Did you know?
Peanut sauce is an original Malayan favourite known as Gado Gado.

cannon balls

A delicious treat to eat instead of sugary commercial sweets.

Makes 12–15

Ingredients	Metric	Imperial	American
Sunflower seeds	*50 g*	*2 oz*	*½ cup*
Almonds	*50 g*	*2 oz*	*½ cup*
Raisins	*50 g*	*2 oz*	*⅓ cup*
Dried dates	*50 g*	*2 oz*	*⅓ cup*
Dried apricots	*50 g*	*2 oz*	*⅓ cup*
Desiccated (shredded) coconut	*50 g*	*2 oz*	*⅔ cup*

1. Put the sunflower seeds and almonds in a blender or food processor and blend until fine. Add the dried fruits and blend for 2–3 minutes more.

2. Form the mixture into balls and roll in the desiccated coconut.

Did you know?
Many dried fruits are treated with chemicals in the drying process. Only eat fruit which has been sun-dried.

pasta, pear and orange salad

Serves 4

Ingredients	Metric	Imperial	American
Sunflower oil	*1 tbsp*	*1 tbsp*	*1 tbsp*
Wholewheat pasta			
* shells*	*225 g*	*8 oz*	*2 cups*
Plain yoghurt	*150 ml*	*¼ pint*	*⅔ cup*
Fruit juice	*5 tbsp*	*5 tbsp*	*5 tbsp*
Chopped fresh mint	*1 tbsp*	*1 tbsp*	*1 tbsp*
Lemon juice	*1 tsp*	*1 tsp*	*1 tsp*
Ripe pears, large	*3*	*3*	*3*
Oranges, peeled,			
* segmented and*			
* roughly chopped*	*2*	*2*	*2*
Fresh mint sprigs,			
* to garnish*			

1.   Add the oil to a large saucepan of water and bring to the boil. Add the pasta shells and continue to boil for about 12 minutes, or until they are just tender.

2.   Meanwhile, mix together the yoghurt, fruit juice, mint and lemon juice.

3.   Wash, core and chop the pears and add them to the yoghurt mixture with the oranges.

4.   Drain the pasta shells and combine with the fruit and yoghurt. Chill before serving in glass bowls, garnished with sprigs of mint.

Did you know?
Pasta comes in many colours. Red pasta is coloured with tomatoes, green with spinach and brown is made from the whole wheat grain. White pasta is made from refined flour. Some parts of Italy even produce a black pasta.

stuffed beefsteaks

Serves 4

Ingredients	Metric	Imperial	American
Beefsteak tomatoes	*2*	*2*	*2*
Cottage cheese	*100 g*	*4 oz*	*½ cup*
Wholewheat breadcrumbs	*50 g*	*2 oz*	*1 cup*
Chopped beetroot	*1 tbsp*	*1 tbsp*	*1 tbsp*

1. Wash the tomatoes and cut the top off each. Using a teaspoon, carefully scoop out the flesh and stand the tomatoes upside down on kitchen paper to drain.
2. In a small bowl, mix together the cheese, breadcrumbs and beetroot.
3. Place the tomatoes on serving plates and fill each with the cheese mixture. Replace the 'caps' and serve with salad.

Did you know?
Tomatoes are classed as vegetables but, botanically, they are really a fruit.

pots of popcorn

Serves 4

Ingredients	Metric	Imperial	American
Popcorn	*100 g*	*4 oz*	*¼ lb*
Soya oil	*1 tbsp*	*1 tbsp*	*1 tbsp*
Clear honey	*2 tbsp*	*2 tbsp*	*2 tbsp*
Sesame (benne) seeds	*2 tbsp*	*2 tbsp*	*2 tbsp*

1.   Put the oil in a large saucepan and heat over a high heat. When hot, tip in the corn and cover with a lid. Shake the pan continuously to prevent sticking ass the corn begins to pop.
2.   When the popping stops, remove from the heat and take off the lid. Stir in the honey until the corn is evenly coated.
3.   Finally, coat the corn with the sesame seeds.

Did you know?
Christopher Columbus discovered corn in Cuba in 1492.

bean and mushroom pate

Serves 4

Ingredients	Metric	Imperial	American
Cooked chick-peas	*100 g*	*4 oz*	*⅔ cup*
Tahini	*1 tbsp*	*1 tbsp*	*1 tbsp*
Chopped onion	*½ small*	*½ small*	*½ small*
Mushrooms	*50 g*	*2 oz*	*½ cup*
Lemon juice, to taste			

1.   Place all the ingredients in a blender or food processor and blend until smooth.
2.   Serve with wholewheat toast or use as a sandwich spread.

CHAPTER 11

friends TO TEA

| *t* | aking and sharing food with others is one of life's greatest pleasures. It is also a marvellous opportunity to show family and friends how delicious wholefood cookery can be.

Good food always tastes just a little bit nicer in attractive surroundings so give some time and thought to presentation. The ingredients you have been using are completely natural, so choose natural containers to show them off. Wooden bowls, baskets and pottery plates will enhance the food far more than a paper plate. Place a small vase of flowers or leaves in the centre of the table, or use dried grasses in winter. Cuttings from the hedgerows laid on a colourful tablecloth also help to create the feeling that you are eating as nature intended.

nutty honey cake

Makes 16 pieces

Ingredients	Metric	Imperial	American
Vegetable margarine	*275 g*	*9 oz*	*1¼ cups*
Clear honey	*6 tbsp*	*6 tbsp*	*6 tbsp*
Brown sugar	*150 g*	*5 oz*	*¾ cup*
Free-range eggs	*4*	*4*	*4*
Self-raising wholewheat flour	*350 g*	*12 oz*	*3 cups*
Chopped mixed nuts	*175 g*	*6 oz*	*1½ cups*
Mixed spice	*1 tsp*	*1 tsp*	*1 tsp*
Lemon juice	*1 tbsp*	*1 tbsp*	*1 tbsp*
Skimmed milk or soya milk	*6 tbsp*	*6 tbsp*	*6 tbsp*

1. Heat the margarine, honey and sugar gently in a saucepan until the margarine has melted. Stir in the eggs one at a time.
2. Mix together the flour, nuts and spice and fold half into the liquid. Stir in the lemon juice and half the milk. Finally, add the remaining flour mixture and milk. The mixture should be of a soft dropping consistency.
3. Spoon into a greased shallow 23 cm/9 inch square baking tin (pan) and bake in a preheated oven at 180°C/350°F/Gas Mark 4 for 55 minutes, or until well risen and firm to the touch. Allow to cool in the tin before turning out and cutting into 16 pieces.

Did you know?
Eating honey produced within a 2-mile radius of home is thought to ease the problems of hay fever.

fresh fruit shortbreads

Makes 8

Ingredients	Metric	Imperial	American
Wholewheat flour	*150 g*	*5 oz*	*1¼ cups*
Brown sugar	*40 g*	*1½ oz*	*¼ cup*
Vegetable margarine	*100 g*	*4 oz*	*½ cup*
Apple jelly	*2 tbsp*	*2 tbsp*	*2 tbsp*
Fresh strawberries, raspberries or blackberries	*225 g*	*8 oz*	*½ lb*

1. Sift the flour into a bowl and stir in the sugar. Using a fork, blend in the margarine until you have a smooth dough.
2. Roll out the dough on a lightly floured surfae to about 5 mm/¼ inch thick. Cut into rounds with a 5 cm/2 inch fluted pastry cutter and arrange on a greased baking sheet.
3. Bake in a preheated oven at 180°C/350°F/Gas Mark 4 for 20–30 minutes, or until just beginning to brown. Leave on the baking sheet to cool.
4. When cold, spread a little apple jelly over each shortbread and decorate with your chosen fruit.

Variations
Any fresh fruit can be used for these shortbreads, and for special occasions you can add fresh cream or Greek-style yoghurt.

Did you know?
Of the English garden fruits, strawberries and blackcurrants contain the most vitamin C.

malty slice

Makes 8 slices

Ingredients	Metric	Imperial	American
Malt extract	1 tbsp	1 tbsp	1 tbsp
Skimmed milk or soya milk	250 ml	8 fl oz	1 cup
Self-raising wholewheat flour	225 g	8 oz	2 cups
Soya flour	50 g	2 oz	½ cup
Brown sugar	50 g	2 oz	⅓ cup
Chopped dried dates	100 g	4 oz	⅔ cup

1. Heat the malt and milk together in a small saucepan until the malt has melted.
2. Place the flours, sugar and dates in a bowl and mix. Make a well in the centre and pour in the malt and milk. Beat thoroughly until all the flour is incorporated.
3. Pour the mixture into a greased 450 g/1 lb loaf tin (pan) and bake in the centre of a preheated oven at 180°C/350°F/Gas Mark 4 for about 1 hour, or until risen and firm to the touch.
4. Remove from the oven and leave to cool slightly in the tin before turning out onto a wire rack to cool completely.
5. When cold, slice and serve with margarine.

Did you know?
Dates are one of the most concentrated sources of natural sugar and natural sugars carry the same health and calorie hazards as refined sugars. So make sure you resist the temptation to eat more than one slice at a time!

peanut and orange squares

Makes 16

Ingredients	Metric	Imperial	American
Vegetable margarine	*175 g*	*6 oz*	*¾ cup*
Brown sugar	*75 g*	*3 oz*	*½ cup*
Orange	*1*	*1*	*1*
Self-raising wholewheat flour	*175 g*	*6 oz*	*1½ cups*
Unsalted peanuts	*100 g*	*4 oz*	*½ cup*
Free-range eggs	*3*	*3*	*3*
Skimmed milk or soya milk	*3 tbsp*	*3 tbsp*	*3 tbsp*

1. Melt the margarine and sugar together in a small saucepan. Beat well and remove from the heat.
2. Grate the orange rind, then peel the orange. Roughly chop the flesh on a saucer so that none of the juice is lost.
3. Place the flour and nuts in a bowl and stir in the orange rind, flesh and juice.
4. Beat the eggs and milk together and pour onto the cool margarine and sugar. Pour the liquid onto the flour and beat well before spooning into a greased and lined 23 cm/9 inch square shallow cake tin (pan).
5. Bake in a preheated oven at 180°C/350°F/Gas Mark 4 for 30–35 minutes or until risen and firm to the touch.
6. Allow the cake to cool slightly before removing from the tin and cutting into squares.

Did you know?
Peanuts are also called groundnuts because they grow close to the ground.

orange and oat slab cake

Makes 16 squares

Ingredients	Metric	Imperial	American
Vegetable margarine	*225 g*	*8 oz*	*1 cup*
Brown sugar	*150 g*	*5 oz*	*¾ cup*
Free-range eggs	*3*	*3*	*3*
Orange juice	*2 tbsp*	*2 tbsp*	*2 tbsp*
Skimmed milk or soya milk	*2 tbsp*	*2 tbsp*	*2 tbsp*
Marmalade	*2 tbsp*	*2 tbsp*	*2 tbsp*
Grated rind of 1 orange			
Rolled oats	*75 g*	*3 oz*	*¾ cup*
Self-raising wholewheat flour	*225 g*	*8 oz*	*2 cups*

1.   Place the margarine and sugar in a bowl and cream together until light and fluffy. Add the eggs, one at a time, beating well after each addition.
2.   Beat in the orange juice, milk, marmalade and orange rind. Carefully fold in the oats and flour.
3.   Spread the mixture evenly in a greased 23 cm/ 9 inch square, shallow baking tin (pan) and bake in a preheated oven at 190°C/375°F/Gas Mark 5 for 35–40 minutes, or until well risen and firm to the touch.
4.   Allow to cool slightly before removing from the tin and cutting into squares.

Did you know?
A small amount of oats added to cakes will help them stay fresh longer.

apple scones

Makes 6

Ingredients	Metric	Imperial	American
Self-raising wholewheat flour	225 g	8 oz	2 cups
Vegetable margarine	75 g	3 oz	⅓ cup
Grated apple	100 g	4 oz	¼ lb
Brown sugar	25 g	1 oz	2 tbsp
Ground cinnamon	1 tsp	1 tsp	1 tsp
Skimmed milk or soya milk	75 ml	3 fl oz	⅓ cup
Milk, to glaze			

1.   Place the flour in a large bowl and rub (cut) in the margarine until the mixture resembles breadcrumbs. Add the grated apple, sugar and cinnamon.
2.   Make a well in the centre of the crumb mixture and pour in the milk. Stir quickly and lightly until you have a soft dough. Gather the dough into a ball and turn out on to a floured surface. Knead gently until smooth.
3.   Roll out the dough to a round 2.5 cm/1 inch thick. Using a 5 cm/2 inch scone cutter, cut out six scones. Arrange evenly on a greased baking sheet and brush with a little milk to glaze.
4.   Bake in the top of a preheated oven at 220°C/425°F/Gas Mark 7 for 10–12 minutes, or until well risen and golden.
5.   Serve with sugar-free blackberry jam.

Did you know?
Cinnamon comes from the bark of a tree. It is available in powder form for baking or in 'quills' for flavouring casseroles, soups or drinks.

sesame and sultana scones

Makes 12–15

Ingredients	Metric	Imperial	American
Self-raising wholewheat flour	450 g	1 lb	4 cups
Vegetable margarine	175 g	6 oz	¾ cup
Sultanas (golden raisins)	150 g	5 oz	1 cup
Sesame (benne) seeds	1 tbsp	1 tbsp	1 tbsp
Brown sugar	50 g	2 oz	⅓ cup
Plain yoghurt	2 tbsp	2 tbsp	2 tbsp
Skimmed milk or soya milk	175 ml	6 fl oz	¾ cup
Milk, to glaze			

1. Place the flour in a bowl and rub (cut) in the margarine until the mixture resembles breadcrumbs. Stir in the sultanas, sesame seeds and sugar.
2. Mix together the yoghurt and milk and pour onto the dry ingredients. Stir quickly with a knife until a soft dough is formed.
3. Turn the dough onto a floured surface and knead lightly. Roll out to a round 2.5 cm/1 inch thick. Using a 5 cm/2 inch pastry cutter, cut out 12–15 scones. Place on a greased baking sheet and brush with a little milk, to glaze.
4. Bake the scones in a preheated oven at 220°C/ 425°F/Gas Mark 7 for 10 minutes, or until well risen.

Did you know?
Plastic-wrapped dried fruits are sometimes coated in an oil to prevent them sticking together. Whenever possible, buy oil-free dried fruits from healthfood shops.

banana loaf

Makes 8 slices

Ingredients	Metric	Imperial	American
Vegetable margarine	*50 g*	*2 oz*	*¼ cup*
Brown sugar	*75 g*	*3 oz*	*½ cup*
Free-range eggs	*3*	*3*	*3*
Large bananas, mashed	*3*	*3*	*3*
Self-raising wholewheat flour	*225 g*	*8 oz*	*2 cups*
Chopped walnuts	*175 g*	*6 oz*	*1½ cups*

1. In a large bowl, cream the margarine and sugar together until smooth and fluffy. Add the eggs, one at a time, beating well after each addition.

2. Beat in the mashed bananas. Stir in the flour and walnuts and beat well.

3. Pour the mixture into a greased 450 g/1 lb loaf tin (pan) and bake in a preheated oven at 180°C/350°F/Gas Mark 4 for about 55 minutes, or until brown and firm to the touch. Turn out onto a wire rack and leave to cool.

Did you know?
You can tell if walnuts are fresh by shaking them before shelling. If they rattle, the nuts are likely to be dry and shrivelled.

banana lollipops

Makes 4

Ingredients	Metric	Imperial	American
Ripe, but firm, bananas	*4*	*4*	*4*
A few drops of lemon juice			
Plain carob bar	*45 g*	*1¾ oz*	*1¾ oz*
Chopped mixed nuts	*50 g*	*2 oz*	*½ cup*

1. Peel the bananas and sprinkle with the lemon juice to prevent discolouration.

2. Break the carob into squares and place in a small bowl with 1 tbsp water. Heat a saucepan of water and stand the bowl on top. Gently stir the carob until it melts.

3. Coat the bananas with the melted carob and roll in the chopped nuts. Place a cocktail stick in each and freeze until required. Alternatively, serve at once if you can't wait to taste them!

Did you know?
Bananas provide you with more energy than most other fresh fruits.

carob brownies

Makes 16

Ingredients	Metric	Imperial	American
Vegetable margarine	*100 g*	*4 oz*	*½ cup*
Brown sugar	*100 g*	*4 oz*	*⅔ cup*
Free-range eggs	*4*	*4*	*4*
Plain yoghurt	*2 tbsp*	*2 tbsp*	*2 tbsp*
Self-raising wholewheat flour	*200 g*	*7 oz*	*1¾ cups*
Carob powder	*75 g*	*3 oz*	*¾ cup*
Chopped walnuts	*50 g*	*2 oz*	*½ cup*
Sultanas (golden raisins)	*100 g*	*4 oz*	*⅔ cup*

1. In a small saucepan, heat the margarine and sugar with 2 tbsp water until the margarine has melted. Remove from the heat and cool slightly.

2. With a wooden spoon, beat in the eggs one at a time, then beat in the yoghurt. Fold in the flour, carob, nuts and sultanas very gently. Mix well and spoon into a lightly greased 23 cm/9 inch square cake tin (pan).

3. Bake in a preheated oven at 180°C/350°F/Gas Mark 4 for about 30 minutes, or until well risen.

4. Leave to cool in the tin, then cut into squares.

Did you know?
Carob is produced by grinding a bean pod. The 'locust bean' grows on trees in parts of Greece.

walnut and raisin bread

Makes 10 slices

Ingredients	Metric	Imperial	American
Self-raising wholewheat flour	225 g	8 oz	2 cups
Rolled oats	25 g	1 oz	¼ cup
Raisins	50 g	2 oz	⅓ cup
Chopped walnuts	50 g	2 oz	½ cup
Skimmed milk or soya milk	150 ml	¼ pint	⅔ cup
Malt extract	2 tbsp	2 tbsp	2 tbsp
Black treacle (molasses)	2 tbsp	2 tbsp	2 tbsp

1. Mix the flour, oats, raisins and nuts together in a large bowl.

2. Gently heat the milk, malt extract and treacle in a saucepan until melted. Leave to cool slightly, then make a well in the centre of the flour and pour in the liquid. Mix well and spoon into a greased 450 g/1 lb loaf tin (pan).

3. Bake in a preheated oven at 180°C/350°F/Gas Mark 4 for about 35 minutes, or until well risen and firm to the touch.

4. Turn out of the tin and allow to cool on a wire rack before slicing. Serve with margarine and some sugar-free jam.

Did you know?
Raisins are dried grapes and, just as you can buy red or black grapes, so you can buy red or black raisins.

drinks

t ea and coffee are by far the most popular drinks taken after meals but, believe it or not, they are relatively new beverages. Our ancestors relied on the herbs of the field for their liquid refreshment. Hot water was poured over all kinds of plants, left to stand for 3–4 minutes and the resulting infusion drunk for pleasure as well as medicinal purposes – verbena for epilepsy, lime for fevers, camomile for nerves and marshmallow root for coughs. There was a plant to cure every complaint.

It now looks as if we have come full circle as experts appear to agree that the vast amounts of tea and coffee we now consume are detrimental to our health. The high levels of tannin and caffeine are contributing to modern diseases. The odd cup is probably okay but it makes sense to offer our youngsters a wide variety of drinks so that they do not become tea and coffee junkies.

To begin with, the fruit or herb teas probably hold more appeal for young palates. Don't be deterred if the first choice is met with groans and moans as the range of teas is vast. My first taste was of camomile, which I loathed, but I discovered there's nothing more refreshing than a mint tea in summer nor more warming than a rosehip tea in winter. Whichever you choose, they are all taken without milk and most benefit from the addition of a slice of lemon. There are also coffee substitutes such as dandelion coffee and Barley Cup as well as the many de-caffeinated coffees.

Most youngsters prefer cold drinks and it really is worth trying to wean them off fizzy, sugary, artificial concoctions. Choose fruit juices with care and look for 'additive-free' labels. Especially avoid the colouring known as E102, or Tartrazine, as it is reputed to cause behavioural problems in certain children. Apple juice concentrate is a healthy alternative as well as economic. Because of its concentration a very little goes a long way.

Lastly, don't forget the most popular drink of all and drunk for thousands of years – cool, fresh, pure water. Alas, our modern tap water can't always be guaranteed pure, so choose one of the many bottled waters or invest in a water purifier.

strawberry ice cream soda

Serves 2

Ingredients	Metric	Imperial	American
Fresh strawberries	*225 g*	*8 oz*	*½ lb*
Low-calorie tonic water	*300 ml*	*½ pint*	*1¼ cups*
Ice cube	*1*	*1*	*1*
Ice cream	*2 tbsp*	*2 tbsp*	*2 tbsp*

1. Reserve two strawberries for decoration. Place all the ingredients in a blender or food processor and blend until smooth.

2. Pour into two glasses and decorate with the strawberries before serving.

Did you know?
Our modern strawberry has evolved from the cross-breeding of berries from Chile and Europe.

fruity refresher

Serves 4

Ingredients	Metric	Imperial	American
Pear	*1*	*1*	*1*
Banana	*1*	*1*	*1*
Mango	*1*	*1*	*1*
Lemon juice	*1 tsp*	*1 tsp*	*1 tsp*
Carbonated water	*300 ml*	*½ pint*	*1¼ cups*
Orange juice	*300 ml*	*½ pint*	*1¼ cups*
Mint sprigs, to decorate			

1.   Wash the fruit. Core the pear, peel the banana and remove the flesh from the mango stone (pit).

2.   Place all the fruit with the lemon juice in a blender or food processor and blend until smooth. Add the water and orange juice and blend again.

3.   Pour into glasses and serve chilled with crushed ice, and decorated with sprigs of mint.

Did you know?
Most canned fruits are full of sugary syrup. It's best to stick to fresh fruits in season.

buttermilk and apricot nectar

Serves 2

Ingredients	Metric	Imperial	American
Apricots, stoned (pitted)	*100 g*	*4 oz*	*1 cup*
Buttermilk	*4 tbsp*	*4 tbsp*	*4 tbsp*
Plain yoghurt	*4 tbsp*	*4 tbsp*	*4 tbsp*
Carbonated water	*300 ml*	*½ pint*	*1¼ cups*

1. Place the apricots in a blender or food processor and blend until smooth.

2. Mix the buttermilk and yoghurt. Add to the blender or food processor with the water and blend.

3. Pour into glasses and serve chilled.

Did you know?
Buttermilk is the liquid obtained during the manufacture of butter and is high in protein but low in fat.

carob cup

Serves 2

Ingredients	Metric	Imperial	American
Skimmed milk or soya milk	600 ml	1 pint	2½ cups
Plain block carob, grated	50 g	2 oz	2 oz
Peppermint extract	½ tsp	½ tsp	½ tsp

1. Heat the milk in a small saucepan. Add the carob and stir until dissolved.
2. Stir in the peppermint and pour into mugs. Serve hot.

Did you know?
Children in Mediterranean countries chew the raw carob bean when it falls from the tree. The taste resembles liquorice.

orange and almond nog

Serves 2

Ingredients	Metric	Imperial	American
Skimmed milk or soya milk	*600 ml*	*1 pint*	*2½ cups*
Ground almonds	*25 g*	*1 oz*	*¼ cup*
Fine oatmeal	*25 g*	*1 oz*	*3 tbsp*
Clear honey	*1 tbsp*	*1 tbsp*	*1 tbsp*
Grated rind and juice of 1 orange			
Free-range egg white, whisked	*1*	*1*	*1*
Chopped mixed nuts	*2 tsp*	*2 tsp*	*2 tsp*

1. Heat the milk gently in a small saucepan.

2. Combine the almonds, oatmeal and honey and add the orange rind and juice. Stir a little of the hot milk into the mixture to thin. Return to the pan and simmer for 2–3 minutes, stirring continuously.

3. Strain the nog into mugs and float half of the whisked egg white on top of each. Decorate with chopped nuts and serve.

Did you know?
Oats are an important source of B vitamins, which have to be replenished every day because the body cannot store them.

index

Additives 7
agar agar..93
Almond munchies 111
almonds..77
'Ants on logs' 129
Apple crumble flan...............90-1
apple juice concentrate 26, 150
Apple scones............................143
apples...................................91, 97
Apricot and apple smoothie...100
apricots..100

Baked bean dip........................125
balanced diet...............................11
Banana fingers, hot..................29
Banana loaf.............................145
Banana lollipops......................146
Banana and sunflower
    cookies 108
bananas...146
basil 129
Bean and mushroom pâté...136
beans 20, 49, 64, 65
    re-fried 125
beansprouts..........................47, 75
    cultivation..............................120
    Oriental......................................75
benne *see* sesame
biscuits...107
black-eyed susies......................68
Black-eyed susies' casserole....68
blackcurrants............................139
Blender breakfast.......................36
breakfasts.......................................21
Brown bread ice cream...........98

brown rice 31
Bubble and beans...................123
Burnham baked beans...........64
buttermilk.....................................153
Buttermilk and apricot
    nectar..153

Cabbage roll-mops...............76-7
cakes..142
calcium.............................13, 61, 31
    in canned tomatoes..............79
    in cheese....................................33
    in chick-peas............................72
    in milk..30
    in sesame (benne) seeds.....110
Cannon balls...........................133
carbohydrates.......................11-12
    simple...12
carob beans.............106, 115, 116,
                                    147, 154
Carob brownies 147
Carob chip cookies 115
Carob cup 154
Carob pears...............................106
Carob pinwheels 112-13
Cauliflower crunch 42-3
cauliflowers..................................43
cereals...9, 25
cheese.................................33, 103
chemical additives.......................7
Cherry and oat cheesecake ...84
chestnuts..53
chick-peas (garbanzos) 59, 72
Chinese stir-fry...........................54
Chips, 'alternative'..................126

cholesterol 54, 73
cinnamon 143
Citrus pancakes 96
Coconut and sesame
    biscuits................................109
colouring for food............88, 150
complex carbohydrates...........12
cookies see biscuits
corn...............................81, 136
corn and tomato, Crumbly....66-7
cottage cheese 50
crêpes *see* pancakes

Dates...140
desserts 83
drinks................................149-50
durum wheat..............................52

Egg and pea scramble.............32
eggs...............................29, 32
energy foods 11-12
equipment 15-16

Fats................................9, 11, 12, 71
    in cheese...................................50
    in peanuts 53
    in sesame (benne) seeds.....12
fibre....................................9, 25, 119
flour 17
Fresh fruit shortbreads 139
fruit................9, 18, 133, 144, 152
    harvesting.................................99
    minerals in 101
fruit and nut bar, No-sugar ...114
Fruit and nut salad 101
Fruity carob flapjacks...........116
Fruity refresher 152

Garbanzos *see* chick-peas
Garbanzos and grains........58-9
gelatine 93
grains 17, 121
Granola......................................25
Grape tart.....................................89
grapefruit 26
    spiced..26
grapes...89
Green and white salad 131

Haricot (navy) beans 80
herbs, medicinal......................149
honey 113, 138
Honey and muesli
    shortbread.............................113
Hummus.......................................72

Ingredients, basic 17-18
iron (mineral) 13, 31, 79

Lasagne, Continental lentil ...78-9
Lemons and limes.........149, 150
Lentil burgers.............................51
Lentil cannelloni 62-3
lentils...............39, 51, 63, 64, 120

Macaroni medley...................56-7
main meals 37
Malty slice...................................140
Meringues, pink and green
    walnut......................................88
Mexican scone pizzas 128-9
milk, skimmed............................30
millet 95
Millet and apricot pudding...95

minerals
    in fruit................................101
    in honey 113
molasses.....................................84
muesli..28
Muesli munch 28
muffins, Morning......................30
Mung bean cottage pie........46-7

Natural sugars....................5, 140
    in dates 140
    in fried onions 45
    in raisins 103
navy beans see haricot
nuts 17-18, 57, 87
Nutty fingers..............................53
Nutty honey cake....................138

Oats 22, 27, 142, 155
oils, vegetable............................18
Onion bundles 127
onions, fried..............................45
Oodles of noodles 52
Orange and almond nog......155
Orange and grapefruit
    baskets....................................85
Orange and oat slab cake....142
Orange oatcakes 27
oranges 85

Pancake parcels.....................48-9
pancakes....................................96
pasta 41, 52, 135
Pasta, pear and orange
    salad...................................134-5
Paupers' potato bake................50
Peach surprise 103
Peanut butter cookies.............117

Peanut dip................................132
Peanut flan.............................86-7
Peanut and orange squares...141
Peanut and raisin cookies...118
peanuts...............................114, 141
    fat content................................53
    protein content 118
    vitamin B 117
pineapple parcels, baked........94
pineapples 94
Pizza pittas 130
polyunsaturated fats................12
porridge, Sultana 22
potatoes...........................125, 126
    Broody................................124-5
Pots of popcorn 136
presentation 37
proteins.......................11, 47, 59
    in almonds 77
    in cottage cheese 50
    in oats.....................................27
    in peanuts.............................118
    in soya....................................61
    in sunflower seeds...............67
pulses...........................18, 19-20
    cooking...............................19, 20
    freezing 20
    growing................................121
Pumpkin and apple
    coleslaw................................122

Raisin slices...........................102-3
raisins 103, 148, 89
raspberries...............................104
Raspberry roll.........................104
Red lentil and apple knobs ...38-9
refined foods.........................7, 24
rice, brown 31

ricotta.............................103
risotto, Rosy.....................65
Roman sausages................69

Salt....................................8
Sarah's fruit pudding.............97
saturated fats.....................12
Saturday savoury pancakes...34-5
sausages............................69
seeds..........................18, 121
semolina....................23, 111
Semolina smoothie................23
Sesame biscuits..................110
sesame seeds and oil.............109
    calcium content..............110
Sesame and sultana scones...144
shoyu...............................35
soya.....................35, 54, 61
Spaghetti bolognese............40-1
strawberries.....................151
    vitamin C content.....105, 139
Strawberry ice cream soda....151
Strawberry and tofu fool......105
Stuffed beefsteaks..............135
sugar.................8, 24, 83, 84
    natural *see* Natural sugars
    reducing use of............83, 101
    refined.......................7, 24
Sultana porridge..................22
Summer fruit charlotte..........99
Sunday brunch.....................33
sunflower seeds.............67, 108
swede, raw.........................74
Swede and potato pie.............74
Sweet swede flan.................44-5

Tahini.........................72, 123
tamari.............................35

Tangerine and rice breakfast...31
Three bean salad..................80
tofu...........................54, 55
Tofu minty pasties................55
tomatoes 9, 130, 135
Tutti frutti trifle..............92-3

Unsaturated fats..................71
Urchins' omelette.................73

Vegetable extract.................39
Vegetable and nut bake.........70-1
vegetables........18, 122, 129, 131
Vegetarian goulash..............60-1
vitamin A..........................12
vitamin B..................13, 36, 31
    in battery eggs...............32
    in oats......................155
    in peanuts...................117
    in yeast extract.............127
vitamin C...13, 85, 89, 104, 105, 139
    in fruit......................99
    in vegetables................131
vitamin D..........................13
vitamin E..................13, 36, 31
vitamin K..........................13
vitamins........................12-13

Walnut and raisin bread.........148
walnuts.......................57, 146
water.............................150
wheatgerm..........................36
wholefoods, definition of..........7

Yeast extract..................39, 127
Yellow mint bricks................81
yoghurt........................24, 98
Yummie yoghurts....................24